UNBROKEN

Thank you, Simone!
Much Love,
   Bethany

UNBROKEN:

A Memoir

By Bethany Granholm

Acknowledgements

This book would never have been if not for Andrea Muller, whose eyes saw this story first, and whose fierce love championed me chapter by chapter to write and then to publish. Thank you, my sister-friend. Thank you to my family, and especially my children, who love me despite everything, and who sacrificed to make this book a reality. Thank you to my friends, whose generous contributions allowed me to bring my story to the world.

A special thank-you is in order to my most amazing team of friends who served as my editors; Anna McCarthy, Rachel Hinton, and my favorite elementary school reading buddy, Tracy Rahn. Your advice and insights proved invaluable. Thank you to my father, Captain Robert Granholm. Dad, you have always been a wonderful father, and I am grateful for you always. A most heartfelt thank-you must also be given to those who made my father who he is - my grandparents Victor and Shirley Granholm. You two have been the first to cheer for my success and the last to comment on my failures. You have been a rock and a helping hand. Words could never be enough. I love you both tremendously.

Finally, thank you to my readers. Thank you for showing me again that love is stronger than fear. The love and support from my community has made me stand taller and stronger.

Life really is better together.

To the eagle, the otter and the owl.

Thank you for bringing me back to life.

Love, your Mama

Why Write A Memoir?

A Foreword

I've always believed that storytelling is a gift, and I've been on the receiving end for most of my life. I read the classics, postmodern works, historical fiction, fantasy, and memoirs, and I loved them all. In my life, stories have been treasures, each one given to me, the reader, to help, to heal, and to entertain. Even when I wasn't the one reading, I was listening. My father is a preacher and my mother is a teacher, and storytelling has been in my blood since the day I came into this world.

Except that, for years I didn't write. I was afraid of my own words, afraid that my terrible truths would spill out for all to read. When I did start writing, I decided to be more academic about it, to put space between my experiences and myself. I wrote about my journey with the desire to piece together my own life on a timeline, and partly to help others with similar struggles, but I feel that I was not actually a part of my story until I started writing about my thoughts, my feelings, and using the word "I". For my story to heal me, I had to own it.

The result of this was that the work, this memoir, became a gift to me. I saw my life from the perspective of a narrator, which was both difficult and freeing, and I began to adopt a more sympathetic view of myself. As I examined my life without judgment, I started to feel a connection to myself as the main character. As I wrote, I found that I was no longer ashamed of myself, but accepting, and in this way the book became a part of my story. Writing was a part of my path to healing.

For almost two years I worked on the manuscript, and while I dreamed of having it published, I was pursuing a degree and raising three young children. Eventually, I put the book away as a project to revisit at a later date. Then, one New Years day, a tragedy occurred that caused me to wonder if my story might positively impact others, and if so, whether or not it was my responsibility to share it. The question I kept returning to was this: If we have hope, is it our duty to give it to those who will accept it from us?

So, with the reader in my mind, I decided to self-publish this memoir. If this book has made its way into your hands, I hope you know that in the end, I wrote it for you. I wish you your own magnificent journey to freedom and wholeness. I pray that you, too, have the help you need to find your way back, and the tools you need to go forward. Most of all, I hope you realize that you are not alone, that you are worthy and deserving of having your own story told, and that if you ever come to a chapter of your own life and think "this is the end," that you will be brave enough to give it one more page. Because if there is hope for me, there is hope for you.

And I hope that now, at the very least, you enjoy what you are about to read.

With Love,
Bethany

CONTENTS

Preface

Some downward spirals are so slow that they creep up on you, taking root in your heart while you are unaware, slowly growing to choke out life. Sorrow winds around your soul until it defines you, until it owns you. You can save yourself only by carefully untangling from the grip of what is crushing you, tediously, painfully, one step at a time, until you are free.

Other times, these spirals are fast and cataclysmic. You lean over the edge of a pit and find yourself at the bottom, surrounded by the debris of your life and the scattered remains of your soul. Then, you take what you can carry and begin the backbreaking ascent to level ground, looking towards the heavens and climbing for your life.

This is how the broken became unbroken.

"When you write your truth,

it is a love offering to the world

because it helps us feel braver

and less alone."

Glennon Doyle Melton, *Carry On Warrior: The Power of Embracing Your Messy, Beautiful Life*

CHAPTER ONE

In The Beginning

My father, having been raised in California during the 60s and 70s, was by nature a most endearing hippie. He was a man given to wanderlust and unplanned adventures. He converted to Christianity in his mid-twenties, after his travels had taken him to the roaring Bible-belt of America. He left home an acid-tripping vagabond and returned home a charismatic, Bible-toting, Billy Graham-quoting preacher. It was a natural combination of his two great loves – God and travel – that drove him to Bible College in Central Canada, and it was not long after starting his Christian education that he fell victim to the destiny of all Bible College attendees. Marriage.

What attracted my father, a man who had grown up in a non-religious home and had lived a fairly liberal life before his great conversion, to a woman like my mother was that she was exactly the opposite.

My mother was adopted as a baby by an elderly couple who could not conceive. Her new mother was a one-room school teacher, and her new father a conservative fire-and-brimstone preacher. My mother had been a Christian as long as she could remember, and had never so much as crossed the street without looking twice.

There was a fear in her, an aversion to recklessness, that, when coupled with her conservative upbringing, managed to keep her far from trouble, although she did dip her toes in wild waters during a summer camp in the late seventies, when she smoked a pack of cigarettes, one after the other so she wouldn't get caught, lighting each one with the end of the one before it and vibrating with the effects of nicotine and rebellion.

By the time my father entered her life, she had repented and made good use of her foolish teenage ways by incorporating it into her personal testimony. Endowed with such righteousness and strength of character, there was no doubt in her mind of her future. She knew just where God was leading her. And my father, who really wanted to get married, knew exactly where God was leading him.

Their wedding was small and uneventful, as my mother's teetotaler parents saw to the reception. The honeymoon was just as uneventful, as I've heard it told, but life was destined to become interesting for both of them shortly after. My parents, misinformed by their expensive religious education, believed that the best way to bring Jesus to the nations was to travel overseas and hand out small, beautifully designed pieces of paper with uplifting Bible verses printed across them. This is exactly what they proceeded to do. My parents joined an organization that traveled in a huge, refurbished tanker ship to any country with an ocean port and a need for Jesus. While my parents lived out their humanitarian dreams, somewhere between Ireland and Venezuela my mother discovered the miracle that is procreation. She was to have a baby.

My mother is a very private individual, and above all, practical. I'd like to think that the news of my impending arrival into this world incited joy and delight in my mother's heart. But it's far more likely that my expected birth was met with a bout of seasickness and a fierce resentment of the man foolish enough to take his new bride to a country with developing-world medical standards. My mother spent her first pregnancy far from her family, far from her home, and far from the shore. She managed to get through this discouraging time by dreaming of the two of us, of nursing me in the sunlight and singing hymns while she rocked me to sleep, this baby that was her ally in the unstable and awkward world of International Missions.

When my mother, who gets sick when she sees blood, heard horror stories from the Venezuelan woman about delivering their own babies in hospital corridors, she urged my father to return to the United States, where his family lived, so that seeing a doctor might be an option. He agreed this was important, and they made arrangements to temporarily leave the mission field. This is how my parents managed to find themselves in Northern California on the finest of midsummer days.

Nestled between California's sprawling coastline and the majestic coastal mountains lies a city filled with Redwood trees and sunshine. It was there, on a hot summer day in mid-July, that my mother began pacing the shag carpet of my grandparents' house, counting contractions and praying through gritted teeth.

My father was away painting the house of the neighbor several doors down, hoping to make enough money to pay hospital fees. This was a fearful concept to my mother, a Canadian with no experience paying for medical services.

She worried about what might happen if they were to show up at the hospital without enough to pay the bill, and since she was in no condition to work herself, she contributed by remaining at home until the end of her long labor, which took her through the heat of the day and into the cool of night.

When it became obvious that medical intervention was needed, my overdue mother was packed into the family station wagon and driven to the hospital, where she was poked and prodded and provided with the luxury of a hospital gurney.

While my mother wondered when it would end, and how much it would cost, my father raced between the delivery room and the waiting room to give ecstatic updates to his parents and his younger sister, who sat for hours in uncomfortable hospital chairs awaiting news. He was so filled with frenetic energy that he made what might be his earliest attempt at a joke.

He ran to the waiting room, scrubs, gloves, and cap on, to inform them that the doctor had fainted and he had delivered the baby himself. He then ran off without another word, leaving them to speculate between themselves about what was happening behind closed doors.

Unfortunately for my mother, the doctor had not fainted. He was wide awake and quite fond of forceps, and when my mother was not successful in managing to deliver me in her own way, he snapped the forceps and cheerfully went to work. That is how one screaming, squalling, purple-faced baby girl came into this world. I was a chubby baby with thick, dark hair that stood straight up on end, like it had been given an electric shock. I was, as my mother was prone to say afterwards, a difficult baby to look at, but my parents managed to recover from this fact and I became the center of their world.

My mother and I were discharged the following morning, and my father came to collect us. We returned to my grandparents' house to find a massive banner stretched across the length of the patio, enthusiastically designed by my politically zealous aunt, which read "Welcome Home Baby, First Female President of The United States!" Sadly, that is not how this story ends, but the sentiment was appreciated by all.

CHAPTER TWO

Lost At Sea

My proud father secured more painting jobs, and my mother settled in to bond with her new daughter. My mother's dream of maternal bliss was short-lived. She nursed me, I cried. She rocked me, I cried. She sang hymns, I cried. She cried, I cried, and together we wrestled with our uniform disappointment with life. I wish I could say now what the problem was, what mysterious issue I struggled with in my tiny body, but the source of my discontent remained hidden from both of us, and my mother unwillingly entered a shift in her job description as she was demoted from Giver of Life to the lesser, more onerous title Holder of The Crying Baby.

As it turned out, there was a limit to my unhappiness, but my mother was rarely the beneficiary of my good moods. By the time my father got home from work, I was tired from a long day of colic. My mother was also tired, and she would hand me to him the minute he got home and shut herself in the bedroom to sleep. I would laugh, coo, and snuggle into my father's sweaty chest to sleep, and that man was never the same because of it. His delight encouraged mine, and from the beginning I was enamored with my father.

My parents returned to the ship and to our exotic lives as missionaries when I was three months old. I spent the next several years bathing in the ocean, running stark-naked across the beaches, and suffering from various unknown tropical diseases while my parents ardently tried to convert the locals.

It was both peculiar and extraordinary to grow up in this part of the world as a child who called a ship cabin and a suitcase home, and I was not the only child there. There were a large number of missionaries on our ship, all with homes and families and churches in other parts of the Western world that provided financial support. We subscribed to an updated version of the Great Commission, one that vaguely translated into "go forth and make disciples of all nations by rendering yourself as literate but poverty stricken, remain uplifted and don't forget to write home and ask for donations." This was the Missionary Way, but all were there with the best of intentions. My life was filled with people who were burdened with bleeding hearts for the nations. I grew up feeling as if this beautiful and tragic part of the world belonged to me.

After several years of living overseas, my parents were weary missionaries. It was early spring when my father was offered work in a real, brick-and-mortar office in Georgia. It was with the same Christian organization that managed our ship. We packed our bags, said goodbye to our ocean home, and headed to the rolling hills of The South.

There is a certain amount of culture shock that occurs when Missionaries return from their post and re-enter their natural culture. There is a feeling of displacement, of not knowing how or where to fit into your old environment after experiencing a more adrenaline-charged version of life and Christianity. This was certainly the case for my parents, who still identified as Missionaries even though they were now living in Georgia. They sought out the familiar church life and re-acclimatized by involving themselves deeply in the local Christian community.

I was also shocked. Georgia was so green and metropolitan that I immediately fell in love with that great southern state. The landscape was marvelously rich, the trees and shrubbery decorated with a kaleidoscope of green, and all of nature was well-manicured and maintained in comparison to the wild foliage of the islands we had left behind. It was breathtaking and beautiful, and it was about to get better.

I was introduced to North America and experienced for the first time things like television, supermarkets, and the great American value of Entitlement. I knew immediately that I was going to enjoy my new home. Now, for the first time in my life, we lived in a house that was our own. We had furniture that was not bolted to a metal floor. I watched a movie for the first time, a Hanna Barbara Bible story, and could not imagine how we had lived without television. I was given my own bedroom, my own toys, and my first pair of brand new shoes, a pair of sparkling red Mary Janes which I prized above all else. I discovered finger paints, bicycles and Strawberry Shortcake. Then I discovered candy. I embraced our new life with all the fervor of a child, thrilled to the core by every new sight and sound, beset with desire and wanting, both literally and figuratively, a five course meal with dessert.

It was in Georgia that I discovered what my parents had known for months – I was going to have a sibling! My sister was born late in the spring, a beautiful baby with rosebud lips and big blue eyes. After enduring me as an infant, my parents braced themselves for the worst, but my pretty baby sister was temperate and manageable, fitting effortlessly into our lives. I loved her from the very start and anticipated the days when she could walk and talk. I would take her under my wing, of course, and turn her into a willing playmate who would never question my creative whims or usurp my authority as the oldest.

I cherished our new life on land, but I also missed the gleaming white tanker ship. I lay awake at night and longed for the ocean air, the continuous jumble of foreign languages, and the rich blue of the sea. I missed the thrill of holding onto the smooth steel railings and seeing nothing but blue ocean stretching out to the white line of the horizon, and the sun, brilliant and everywhere, radiating a warmth that reached down into your bones. I dreamt of sailing through the deep on my ship, leaving white-capped waves behind as we parted the sea on the way to the next adventure.

This dream was not meant to be. Not long after my sister was born, the ship was traveling in the South Pacific when it became trapped in a raging tropical storm. It ran aground, and though all were safely evacuated, the ship itself could not be recovered. It sits there now, mostly underwater, just miles off the Chilean coast, broken atop the rocks it ran aground on. The once-beautiful vessel is now a rusted carcass of its original form, red and jagged against the lush green of the coast. She sits as a monument to brokenness, raising her crumbling face to heaven, mocking the dreams of short-term missionaries everywhere and reminding all who view her that even on the surest course, storms come and we can find ourselves astray.

Our life in Georgia came to an end when my father received another job opportunity, this time in the strange land of Canada. It was the nineties, and there was a new missionary dream, a more systematic approach. No longer were missionaries content to travel the world and deliver literature. This new organization wanted to gather educated, missions-minded individuals, those with careers and transferrable skills, and send them to countries with the highest population of Muslims. From Morocco to China, they would "plant" their missionaries, encouraging them to build lives, to have families, and to live among those they were ministering to, going undercover as school teachers and business owners while attempting to convert Muslims by leading shining examples of Christian lives. Never one to turn down the chance to move, my father accepted and we packed our considerably larger bags and made our way up the Eastern seaboard, eventually settling in Ontario.

There, my parents welcomed another daughter, a delicate, fair-haired, blue-eyed baby with a delightfully pleasant disposition. Not overly creative with nicknames, I called her Baby, and the name stuck for several years, until she put her tiny little foot down and demanded to be called by her rightful name.

Expert scheduling was the glue that kept our growing family together, and I learned to appreciate the word "Agenda". On Wednesdays, my mother and I would bake cookies while my younger sisters napped, enjoying our homemade treats on bean bag chairs while watching *The Cosby Show,* the only daytime television my mother approved of. On Saturdays, my father would take me to the local diner for breakfast, and we could eat our pancakes at the counter, sitting between the bikers as they smoked their cigarettes while eating their bacon and eggs. During the week, I was homeschooled by my mother, who dedicated many hours of her life teaching me to paint, draw, and read.

One of the drawbacks of our interesting lives as missionaries was that, as children, we didn't have the time or ability to develop close friendships. It was my family with whom I had the most in common, our specific set of life experiences creating a bond that became increasingly important as we grew older. Whom could I identify with, other than my sisters? When our relationship became strained by things like tantrums and irritating personal habits, such as whining, I drew back in solitary retreat. To compensate for what was lacking in my life, I developed an imaginary friend, an invisible dairy cow, to whom I would feed pinecones as we sat and discussed current events in my family life.

Just as my mother had finished unpacking from our move to Ontario, my father received another job offer. He was needed on the West coast to take the position of Director for the new head-office of the missions organization, and once again, we started packing. My father drove our things in a U-haul truck across Canada, dreaming of Saddam Hussein's great conversion to Christianity, while my mother got to make the trip out west on a plane, with an infant, a toddler, and myself.

She prayed for all our souls while I hopped on and off the vacant seats, paging the stewardess for orange juice at each one. Just as my mother began to wonder if she could be forgiven for getting off the plane without me, I saw the EXIT sign. I plunked myself down into the empty seat next to it and read the words "Pull to Release". And that is exactly what I did.

I didn't have enough strength to get the door open, but the alarm did sound and an angry stewardess returned me to my mother and buckled me into my seat for the duration of the flight. My mother looked like she wished the door *had* opened to swallow me whole, but despite her hopes and dreams, we arrived in Vancouver all together and my father arrived to take us to our new home.

After our move to the West coast, my parents decided it was best if I was no longer home-schooled. I was sent to a Christian elementary school, where I experienced the thrill of falling in love for the first time. This lucky young man was the handsome son of a local television evangelist, but, sadly, he did not return my affections. My first boyfriend spent the entirety of our week-long relationship running from me while I tried to chase him down.

"Hands to yourself!" my teacher admonished, and I took this to mean *hands-free kissing*. My first in-school time-out was for kissing a boy until he cried.

These years were full of good memories and great friends, but it was the relationship with my father that meant the most. He woke me up in the early morning, made my breakfast and my lunch, drove me to school on his way to work, and picked me up on the way home. During the school year it was my father with whom I spent the most time, and we kept our Saturday morning routine of going out for breakfast, although by this time my younger sisters were also invited, and we'd given up breakfast diners in favor of McDonald's. On Sunday, we attended church as a family.

There was no life, no concept of life, outside our Christian community. We lived inside a safe bubble, a good Christian family, going to a good church and a good Christian school, with my mother managing Sunday school and my father working in missions.

I was taught to pity the outside world, the non-Christians who lived miserable lives without a Lord and Savior. It was never the wrong time to quote scripture to a stranger, especially if they happened to be drinking or smoking or talking about evolution. The worst were the non-Christians who were happy. They were to be feared, because we never knew what sin was in their hearts. We didn't talk to them. Those ones made the prayer list. It was us and them until the end of time, or until the rapture, if you went to our church.

CHAPTER THREE

Me And My Girlfriend

There was a shift in our family dynamics when, eventually, I made friends at school. My parents had a firm no-sleepover rule, so after-school play dates became the pinnacle of my elementary school life.

It was amazing to me when I discovered that my friends had different lives than mine. I was curious and inquisitive, eager to investigate the way they lived and enjoying the chance to be a part of someone else's day in their own environment.

A friendship was sparked between myself and another little girl in my class. We had been paired up several times for group assignments, so to me, with my limited experience of long-term relationships, it seemed like we had known each other for a very long time. She was lithe and energetic, with long red hair and a confidence that came from the familiarity of living all her life in one place. She was the antithesis of who I was, and it fascinated me.

When I was first invited to her house after school, I was completely unprepared for what awaited me. Her house was the largest I'd ever been in, a massive structure with a completely white interior that shone as the sunlight came through all the many large, undressed windows. It was so beautiful. I was bewitched, and that was only the beginning. We were served potato chips and canned pop, two things my mother never let darken the door of her kitchen, and when her mother suggested that we take our snack to the living room and watch *Saved By The Bell*, I took my wide-eyed self and got comfortable on the big white couch, grinning from ear-to-ear at the television screen.

I correctly presumed that my mother would never let me out of the house again if she knew that I'd spent hours watching forbidden television shows and eating especially forbidden foods. I wisely kept this to myself when she asked how my day had gone.

"But what did you do?" asked my mother, after getting an unsatisfactory response.

I shrugged and replied uncertainly, "We just...played?"

When she looked at me like she wanted a more descriptive report, I patted my stomach and said "Wow, I'm hungry. I sure would like a piece of multi-grain toast!"

And that was the end of the interrogation.

I was happy to go back there, to that big house with the white marble floors, with the white staircase that curved around at the end and the plush white carpet that felt like a dream. It was such a different home than mine. We rented across town in a neighborhood that was older and more suburban, and at *my* house my little sisters were there, which ruined the magic as far as I was concerned.

At the white house, there was not only space inside but outside as well, as it was situated in the middle of several acres of flat, green land, bordered by trees and a road not often used. When we wanted to play outside, it was possible to run and shout and scream and not see another person for hours, or until her mother called us in.

It was on one of those days, a day spent outside in the warm, slow afternoon, that I experienced my first real kiss. Until then, the only kissing I'd done had been with the unfortunate boy at school, who ran from me every time I pursed my lips. It was memorable, definitely diary-worthy, but this time was different in every way.

My friend and I had come upon a discarded wooden trailer, and we climbed up on it to lie down in the sun as we talked. It tilted so that it faced away from the house and balanced on the ground at the hitch, with the flat part facing the afternoon sun. When I leaned back I had to shut my eyes to avoid being blinded. We were laying there talking about the upcoming track and field event at school when suddenly the sun was no longer in my eyes, and when I opened them, there was her face, inches from mine, her long hair hanging like a curtain around my head.

When her lips touched mine, it was like an electric shock ran through my body. I startled and she drew back slightly, but as I looked into her expectant face, her eyes sparkling with excitement as she hovered above me, something in me lit, and I drew closer to her and kissed her back.

If questionable food and entertainment required secrecy, so much more did our esoteric friendship. I weighed my parents reaction in my mind and knew that it was best to hide, even if I didn't know why. I only knew that I wanted to come back, to relive that moment over.

And so it went, both of us intensely guarding our secret and our desire to be alone again, until things turned a corner that I did not see coming.

We were in her bedroom that day, eating our after-school snack and playing with her dolls. I was holding a Barbie and a handful of cheezies when she suggested that we go outside.

"We should go play in the barn today," she said, shifting around restlessly on the floor. "There's a secret place I need to show you!"

Nothing could have been more tempting, more seductive, than a secret place. Since I'd started reading novels, my hunger for adventure and delicious secrets had grown with my imagination.

Ever the optimist, I wondered if this secret place was a sunlit room full of interesting books and antique jewels, maybe a fur coat or two and a stash of bubble gum. She bolted out the door and down the stairs, and I ran behind her, licking the orange cheese residue from my fingers on the way.

We entered the barn through a small door on the northern side, adjacent to the main doors. I followed her up a wooden staircase to an upper level where it looked like there was nothing but cubed bales of hay tied together. We got to the top and ventured through a narrow opening where the rows of hay didn't go completely to the side of the building. I found myself in a clearing, the hay bales serving as a wall, obscuring vision and noise from downstairs and outside.

It was darker than the rest of the barn, with almost no natural light. She turned on a light bulb that hung from an electrical cord that was tightly wrapped around a ceiling peg, and as my eyes adjusted I could see that the air was thick with dust. It was uneasy there. The feeling clung to me like a jacket that just didn't fit, tight and uncomfortable in important places. I didn't know if we should stay or if we should leave.

As my friend began to kick some loose hay on the wood floor, she looked up at me and motioned me over with her arm.

"What are we doing?" I whispered, unsure if I should be making any noise.

She smiled, and before I could say anything more her mouth was on mine, and seconds later she had taken off my shirt in one expert maneuver. A few minutes later, all our clothes were on the floor.

What I remember about that afternoon was the strange push-and-pull that occurred between us. It was as if every move I made interfered with what she was doing. If I tried to move left, she would steadily guide me to the right. There was no softness to her touch, and neither was there roughness, but a firm and guided caress that moved my hands here, my body there. She was surprisingly skillful, never pausing to discuss or question what would happen next.

It made me anxious and insecure. I knew with everything in me that I was playing a part in a grander scheme that had been intentionally hidden from me, and that my dear friend had brought me here knowing, but not saying, what was going to transpire.

Later on that night, when I was lying awake mulling over the events of the day, my body began to shake and grow cold. I wanted to figure out what had happened, I wanted to know everything, to think about it until it made sense, but my body was at war with my anxious mind. I felt nauseous and frozen. *Don't think about it. Don't talk about it. It's not real if I don't remember it.* I thought to myself. I decided that I would carry on as if this never happened, but in the future I planned to decline further invites to her house.

This foresight was not necessary, as I was never invited back. The next week she had a new best friend, and I tried to follow her example and found new friends myself. But there was a widening gulf now, between myself and the other girls at the school, and though I desperately wanted friends I was never sure who was safe, and who was going to bring me into their confusing and secret world.

When my mother noticed that the two of us were no longer as close as we had been, I told her with the utmost sincerity, "She is always drinking pop and watching teenage tv shows. I don't know if I want to be her friend."

My mother nodded in agreement, and the conversation ended with both of us feeling like I had uncovered and absorbed a valuable life lesson.

"...we long for our churches to be safe places to doubt, to ask questions, and to tell the truth, even when it's uncomfortable...

we want to bring our whole selves through the church doors, without leaving our hearts and minds behind"

Rachel Held Evans, *Searching For Sunday: Loving, Leaving, and Finding the Church*

CHAPTER FOUR

Blessings Come

I was in grade four when my father inherited some money, and my parents agreed the time had come to buy their first house. They couldn't afford to purchase a home in the city where we were living, so they started looking in more rural areas, and I started packing to move. Like all our moves before, the change was not unwelcome. Yet this time, instead of another adventure, I saw our move as a chance to start fresh, the opportunity to rewrite the occasionally unpleasant experiences of my early elementary school years.

My father found for our family a three-level townhome on a lot towards the back of a dead-end street. It was enclosed on three sides by a green belt and a gully, far from all traffic on the outskirts of our new home town. Unlike our old life in suburbia, surrounded by fences and roads and neatly carved bicycle paths, this area was wilder, more unencumbered. We had an open backyard with an uncharted forest full of rivers and underbrush, waiting for forts and secret platforms to be built, platforms from which my sisters and I could spy on our neighbors.

In many ways this move was the new beginning I had been hoping for. My sisters and I began the next year in a new school, my parents joined a new church, and my father, while still working in missions, decided that he would like to start his own business. He enlisted the help of his friends and together with my father's money and his friend's craftsmanship, they started a roofing company. The business started successfully, and by wintertime my father had signed contracts and started shingling roofs.

My sisters and I were waiting to be picked up from school on a particularly cold day when my mother arrived, so late that the gates to the school property had almost been locked up. I threw my backpack into the front seat and gave her my long list of complaints – I am *starving!* I had to wait *outside!* With *my sisters!!* – but before I got to the worst part, my mother burst into tears.

She had just come from the hospital, she explained, where my father was in surgery. He had fallen off a roof after losing his footing on ice, plunging feet-first off the edge of the roof and landing on a cement plot. Miraculously, he survived, but he had shattered his ankle.

It was unnerving to see my mother so upset, and the news of my father's accident horrified us all. We went directly to the hospital to wait for news, but when we did see my father he was so full of morphine that he barely moved. We returned home with fear inside our hearts, and I spent an anxious night pleading with God not to take my father from me.

The prognosis, while not fatal, was not reassuring. Surgery had gone well, but infection had set in. When the infection had cleared, more surgery was required. Bones were re-broken and reset and re-broken again until my weary father at last returned home, cast on, to spend his days on a bed in the middle of our living room, unable to walk.

My sisters and I tried our best to entertain him. We would come home from school and put on wild plays and concerts, directed and executed by myself. We would don wigs, dress up in costume, throw streamers around the living room. My father would smile and nod and try to stay awake while we attempted to cheer him up. Over time it became obvious to him that he might be subject to home productions of The Christmas Story for years upon end, and one day he decided he would make more progress in a live-in physiotherapy center.

He arrived at his temporary new home in a wheelchair, and six weeks later walked out with a cane, which he was told he would need all his life. It was recommended that my father find a new career. He made arrangements to return to Bible College, this time to get ordained as a Minister. My father said goodbye to manual labor and returned to his desk at the Missions Organization, recruiting missionaries, studying in his spare time, and travelling when able.

My father was on a flight home from one of his trips when his scheduled stop-over was delayed. Stranded at the airport with his travelling companions, he remembered hearing reports of a wild evangelical church located at the airport they were now in. A church which had developed a reputation among the more conservative churches as a place of "revival and restoration," two things traditional minds are wary of.

They agreed amongst themselves that this church should be investigated. In pain and exhausted from his recent trip, my father borrowed a wheelchair from the airport and entered the ongoing church service just in time to hear the speaker announce that there would be a prayer of healing for everyone in the building who suffered from physical ailments.

No one, not even my father, can say for certain what occurred right then, but the fact remains that he got out of his wheelchair, ran around the large convention-sized room, and never had a use for his cane again. Whether or not he was misdiagnosed, or whether he was supernaturally healed, that man found the strength to stand when he should sit, to run when he should walk, and to let go of the crutch he no longer needed. That in itself is an undisputed miracle.

He returned home with a renewed passion for life, and it was a few months later when my parents announced another miracle: they were expecting a baby!

With a husband in school and a baby on the way, my mother figured she'd better get herself a job. Our church was looking for a youth pastor, someone to corral and encourage the younger generation, the gum-chewing, walkman-carrying rebel-rousers who preferred to sit on bleachers rather than a cold church pew.

Our church did not support women in leadership positions, but my mom got around that by applying for the job, not the title, and she was hired as the young adult leader.

Her new role brought out personality traits I'd never known existed beneath her conservative armor. Young Adult Leader Mom was fun, creative, and slightly eccentric, and while this attracted the youth at our church it irritated me to no end. How dare she be so interesting! I suspected that my mother had intentionally chosen a career that ensured she would be able to keep me within arm's reach. I felt suffocated and scrutinized, and now my peers had a front row seat to the strained relationship between my mother and I, a relationship in which I played the villain.

I was angry at my mother. I was angry at my friends who loved my mother. I was angry at the church for hiring my mother. I was angry at God, who had clearly misunderstood our family prayers and couldn't find the time to divinely direct my mother to the "We're Hiring!" sign at the local grocery store. Anger became an essential ingredient in my life, one I carried around in my pre-teen body like a weapon.

My father noticed, and he advised me to channel all my negative emotions into a craft – why not writing? he suggested. To encourage me, he bought exquisite journals, leather-bound books full of hand-pressed pages. Appealing to my antiquated flair for drama, he gave me the gift of a blown-glass inkwell and fountain pen, and with these treasures I began my amorous affair with the written word.

He also prompted me to open a bank account and to start a paper route. He believed that financial autonomy was the equivalent of independence for certain people, such as myself, who struggled with authority but could not function in society on their own. Armed with this good advice, I ventured out into the world of gainful employment, and found that it was true; I *did* like having my own money.

My father and I were at the bank one rainy Saturday afternoon so I could get money from my account for a school fair. The teller prepared the statement and handed me my coins, but on the way out I noticed that she had given me twice what she had written on the receipt. I showed my father, who said the error was the fault of the bank teller and that I wasn't obligated to return the money, but that I should do what I thought was right.

I returned to the bank and made my way to the back of the line. When I came back outside, with less money and a lighter conscience, my father nodded approvingly and said "This may seem like a little thing you just did, but blessings come when you do the right thing. Just wait and see – something good is around the corner!"

The following evening we were at the dinner table when the phone rang. My mother answered, and it just happened to be a good friend of hers, a friend who was looking for a hard-working, energetic, eleven-year-old girl to help with light housekeeping and yard work at her hobby farm.

I looked at my father with wide eyes, and he tilted his head towards mine and said "Consider it! Remember what I said yesterday – this might be the blessing you are owed!"

My mother arranged for me to start the next weekend. Overjoyed, I excused myself from the table to go and write in my journal, making a list of all the things I would be able to afford with two jobs. A paper route and a weekend job, boy was I going to be rich!

I arrived at the farm with my hair up and my purse open. It soon became clear that cleaning was not one of my top career options, but in yard work, I found my calling. The couple I worked for were expectant, but not demanding. Things were thoroughly explained and then I was left alone to weed-whack blackberry bushes and mow the fair-sized lawn from the top of a ride-on John Deere.

The vigor with which I attacked my new job surprised everybody, including myself, but I found a sense of calm and connectedness from being outside. I spent all day with my hands in the earth and my head in the clouds, and I enjoyed it so much that the whole time I worked there, I never bothered to ask what I was being paid.

The summer arrived and brought my baby sister into this world. My other two sisters had been born when I myself was still a child, so our sibling relationship was more a camaraderie, but my baby sister ignited my maternal instinct and I loved her more than I ever loved anyone. It was in caring for her that my own dream of motherhood began, and I often imagined myself with my husband by my side as I held my precious first born child in my arms, a birth so momentous it would become the occasion by which all other milestone events would be measured.

My parents felt that it was their duty to prepare me for a life of motherhood by appointing me as de facto babysitter. I was not to be compensated for this, because servitude was its own reward, and in truth I did love being the temporary boss and I loved being with my baby sister.

This changed, however, when I realized you could be *paid* for babysitting. I discovered this while reading a *Babysitters Club* book. By the time I had turned the last page, I had formulated my own business plan.

My mother enrolled me in a Red Cross first-aid course, and I made myself business cards and flyers, which I tucked into the papers from my paper route and delivered door-to-door.

I stapled pull-tabs with my phone number to telephone poles and made posters, which I taped over the top of bus stop advertisements.

My father breathed a long sigh of relief as I bounced around like a cheerful pinball, springing awake each morning and catapulting into school, various jobs, and slightly less enthusiastically, our church life.

CHAPTER FIVE

Learning A New Language

The farm was owned by a Christian couple, religious enthusiasts who dedicated their life to spreading the Word of God. A sudden downpour once forced me inside during the middle of painting the shed, and I sat in front of the television to casually watch a movie about Satan and the Illuminati while I waited out the storm. Other weather-related delays saw me licking stamps and affixing them to hundreds of packages of Christian pamphlets, on their way around the world to bring light to dark places.

It only made sense that they would host religious meetings on their acreage, using their blessings to bless others. They welcomed all manner of Christians, even the liberal minded, who they were sure to convert to the narrow path of righteousness. These home-church services attracted a crowd, many of them families with young children, and someone needed to watch these children while the adults tended to their own salvation. I saw an opportunity to present my babysitting business card.

I was hired.

I was expected to keep the children quiet and out of the way until the end of the service, when we would all reconvene in the kitchen to enjoy delicious treats, provided by the women who engaged in an unspoken bake-off. I left the meetings with money in one hand and a pie in the other, which has always been my preferred method of payment.

One evening, a couple came to the meeting that I had never met before. Their love story was exemplary. She had gone to Israel to convince the Jews of the merits of Christianity, and had met, and subsequently converted, a handsome young local. They got married, got pregnant, and returned to Canada to raise their young daughter. It was easy to see why he had fallen in love with her. She was beautiful with a pliant demeanor, the embodiment of all he held dear. She saw only the good in him, a habit cultivated by her religious upbringing and by the belief that love could conquer all.

I met him for the first time when he brought his infant daughter to meet me for childcare. Other than his penchant for tapered jeans and running shoes, there was nothing remarkable about him that made our first meeting memorable. Rather, it was his daughter who stole the show. She was, with the exception of my own baby sister, the most beautiful little girl. She had large, dark eyes that were framed with the longest and thickest of lashes. Her black hair hung in glossy ringlets, smooth and soft as silk. Her chubby little hands wound around my neck and she stayed in my arms all evening.

Her father noticed, and when they came back the next week he offered to stay with me, concerned that I wouldn't have enough time to watch the other children if I was always with a baby on my lap. He sat with me, making conversation by trying to convince me of the merits of marrying a foreigner.

"I have a younger brother back home," he said, "He's only fifteen but age really doesn't matter."

"Fifteen is still too old for me!" I told him, and he shook his head in disagreement. The conversation turned to other things, but before the meeting was over, he put his hand on the top of my head and leaned in to say,

"I'm going to start teaching you my language. You never know when you will need another tongue." Then he turned, with a wink, to leave.

He did as he said, and in the ensuing weeks he would follow me, corner me when he could, and stand inches from my face while he repeated word after unfamiliar word. He was very serious about this task, and I couldn't walk away or even turn around until I had repeated both the word he was trying to teach me and the English meaning. I was often wrong, but when I correctly pronounced the vocabulary word I was rewarded with a kiss.

I hesitantly brought this up to one of my friends at school, who agreed that this was unusual and urged me to tell my parents and maybe even refuse to babysit.

Neither of these options sounded good to me. In my family, we went to great lengths to avoid embarrassing conversations, and I didn't want to force unpleasant discourse if I could help it, especially because the relationship with my mother had become increasingly turbulent and uncomfortable. How could I tell them, and if I did, how could I explain why I'd let him kiss me? I couldn't.

I didn't want to refuse to babysit, either. I loved the farm and I loved my employers. I didn't want to have it all taken from me if it turned out I'd made too much of nothing.

I turned the problem over in my mind and decided that the best course of action was to wait it out, hoping that maybe he would stop coming to the meetings, or that maybe he would stop trying to teach me a new language. There were a lot of ways to solve this, I thought, and the less people who knew about it, the better.

It was a crisp fall evening, and I was wearing jeans and a hooded sweatshirt. The number of people who came to the Christian meetings had nearly doubled now that the summer was over, so the Children's Meeting, as my growing childcare group was called, now took place downstairs. That night, I was in the kitchen eating potato pancakes when people started to arrive. I hurriedly took my supplies for the evening downstairs to organize the room before the children came down.

I was setting out board games and coloring pictures when the hair on the back of my neck stood on end. I knew without turning around that it was him. When I turned to face him, he said nothing, but lowered his eyelids and gave an eerie nod.

He stood there, with eyes narrowed and arms motionless at his side. He watched me, waiting to assess my reaction to the situation. I began to calculate my movements, shuffling slowly around the coffee table, but it made no difference. It was just entertainment for him. He was waiting for me to run. I saw it in his eyes.

I sat down on the couch and awkwardly motioned towards the coffee table, pointing to the monopoly game as an explanation for what I had been doing. He jerked forward and moved past the table, never breaking eye contact. I wanted to look away, to see anything else, but I was terrified that he would move faster if I wasn't watching him. He stopped directly in front of me.

"It's time for your lesson," he snarled, his words thick and venomous. He moved his hand and put his finger lightly on my lips, drawing my mouth. He leaned closer and spoke a word I couldn't understand. His mouth was only inches from mine, and I could feel his breath on my face. He inhaled and moved his head to the side of mine, whispering in my ear, "Say it."

I slid myself further onto the couch, trying to create distance between us so that I could answer. It was a trap, that I knew, but the intensity of the situation made me nervous and I couldn't think of a way to respond. I looked up at the ceiling, tears in my eyes, and shakily replied, "I, I ca-can't."

"Say it," he commanded, "Be a good girl, repeat the lesson and you'll be rewarded."

I tried to move away from him, but he had stretched his hands out on either side of my body so that the only way to avoid touching him was to lean back so that I was directly underneath him. He looked down at me, his dark eyes filled with contempt. His glare was so frightening that I could not look away. I tried to search his face for intent, trying to find a purpose to this, but I saw nothing but anger. There we were, staring into each other's eyes, me trapped beneath the weight of his hatred, and him, waiting for an answer.

It came to me suddenly, the word. I repeated what he had said correctly. He broke eye contact and drew back, and taking this small gesture as a sign of retreat, I took a deep breath and relaxed, shifting my weight onto one elbow and positioning my other hand to push off the couch the moment he gave me enough space to maneuver.

It wasn't until I looked up at his face again that I knew I had made a mistake. He was livid, his face flushed and covered with sweat. His eyes were wild now, full of frightening desire, something I misunderstood as the desire to murder. I wanted to close my eyes but terror kept them wide open. My mind screamed at me to run, to claw, to fight, to scream, but my body went rigid, unresponsive to my need for escape. I was frozen. My mind, realizing a crisis was at hand, developed a plan. My consciousness withdrew, leaving this nightmare behind as it traveled into a better dream. It was only my body that remained.

Upstairs, there was the rustling of footsteps, and then the music started. I felt my long hair pulled down, bringing my head to the couch cushion. I felt his wet hair on my face, his hands on my body. I heard the sound of tambourines, the worship from above. I didn't know if I was breathing. I didn't even know if I was there.

The figure before me grew taller, darker. I heard his belt buckle come undone, and I heard it when his whitewashed Levi's were unzipped. *I wonder if they know,* I thought to myself as he unbuttoned my jeans. I tried to imagine the people upstairs, but everything was too blurry inside my head.

I began to ponder the mysteries of the ceiling above me, to wonder why certain spots were where they were. He tried to pry my legs apart as he fumbled with my jeans, but I had crossed my feet at the ankles and my tense body would not be manipulated, not by him. Fury and urgency took over, and he stood above me, pumping and swearing and spraying me with spit and rancor.

He finished, and I still did not move. My bare stomach was sticky and wet, little rivulets making their way down the side of my body like tears. He dressed while I watched him from the corner of my eye, still paralyzed. He took in the sight, me on the couch, pants undone, shirt above my chest, my navel filed with a pool of semen. He wiped up one of the rivulets and laughed, kissed me on the mouth, and wiped his wet fingers across my face, walking back upstairs to join his wife and daughter as they sang songs to the Lord.

CHAPTER SIX

Book Burning

Propelled by an inner voice that demanded action, I came alive and hurried to the downstairs bathroom. I clutched my stomach like I had been wounded, trying to contain the liquid so that it didn't drip onto my clothes that were, mercifully, still on my body. I kicked the bathroom door open and kicked it closed. I locked the door, then unlocked it, and then locked it again. A terror had crept into me. I feared that he would return, or that he hadn't really left, and that he was waiting for me in some dark corner of the house.

I turned on the hot water in the sink and rinsed my hands, then turned on the shower. I watched the steam fill the room and longed, more than anything in that moment, to stand under the stream of scalding hot water, to go in and never come out.

But I knew that upstairs the children were playing unsupervised. If I did not return to usher them downstairs, my absence would be noticed and an explanation required. I slowly turned the water off and looked around for soap. Finding a jar of face wash, I slathered it over my stomach and wiped it off with a towel, comforted by the pharmaceutical smell that filled the air.

I rearranged my clothes and reached for the door handle, but I was so overwhelmed with fear that my hands began to shake and when the door wouldn't open I began to panic. I struggled against it, silent tears streaming down my face. Then I realized that the door was still locked. My mind instructed my hands to open the door, but my hands refused. I stood there, warring with myself, demanding that I open the door, when suddenly a strange calm filled my being, and without hesitancy I opened the door and went upstairs to the meeting, feeling and believing that nothing out of the ordinary had just occurred.

This overwhelming feeling of panic and terror, followed by a detached calm, became my reality. The pendulum would swing from the apex of emotions and then retreat to an utter lack of them. These shifts were unpredictable and terrifying, brought on when I was triggered by a memory, such as a similar couch or a man who tucked his shirt into his jeans, or by a feeling, such as confusion or fear. When I was erratic and emotional, I became angry, brooding, and distrustful of everyone. I would analyze my experience in that basement over and over in my mind, trying to fit together pieces that I couldn't understand and had no vocabulary for.

The unanswered questions ate at me, trapping me in my own memories. Panic and anxiety twisted and churned, trying to escape. Then my unchecked emotions would tip and the floodgate doors would shut, and no emotion remained.

This went on for months, and it was only I who knew the reason. I continued to babysit for the meetings, although I had requested that child care take place upstairs in the piano room.

I would hold his daughter in my hands, sometimes crying into the back of her soft curls, curls that were like his, winding around her face like a black ribbon.

I avoided him when I could, and when I could not I looked through him with a stony gaze. Eventually, he and his wife stopped attending meetings. I should have been glad when I arrived one week to find he was not there, and I was, but the change created a paranoia that I could not overcome. I was accustomed to seeing him in one place and one place only, and when he was not in that place, I began to fear he would find me somewhere else instead.

This fear followed me everywhere. I would lay awake at night, my back flat against the bed, afraid that he was on the other side of my closed bedroom door. I imagined him climbing through my bedroom window, which was so large it took up the length of a wall. I became afraid of everything dark. I feared the night, black dogs, men with dark hair, cars with tinted windows, a passerby with a dark hooded jacket.

As the winter months closed in and night came earlier, I became afraid of my paper route. One day, with no apparent consideration, I refused to deliver papers. My mother assumed that I was acting out in rebellion and fought with me over my sudden decision. She locked me out of the house until the papers were delivered as usual, sure that a little tough love would cure my errant ways.

I got on my bike and pedaled furiously until I reached the other side of town. Exhausted, I stopped at a friend's house just as they were sitting down to dinner, and my friend's well-meaning mother called my parents to see if I could stay.

Ten minutes later, my father was in their driveway. He was frustrated.

"What is the problem with the paper route?" he asked, concerned that I was showing a tendency to secede before seeing something through.

"I don't want to do it. I hate being outside." I responded.

"Sometimes, we just have to do things we don't want to do." he explained.

I responded with silence, and we drove home with me choking back my rage and indignation.

I was at the tail-end of my pre teen years, and because of this my behavior was attributed to hormones and rebellion. My parents reacted to this in opposite ways.

My mother believed that the problem lay in my heart, that my bad attitude could only be corrected by nipping defiance in the bud. Her discipline, borne out of her conservative worldview, took the form of rules and punishment. No makeup. No dating. No magazines. No non-Christian music. No sleepovers. No more babysitting. I was not to be alone with my sisters, lest my rebellious ways catch on. I was not to accept invitations to events, outings, or birthday parties unless she could accompany me, and there were to be no friends over until I could control my boiling ire.

My father, blessed with a more liberal childhood, reflected on his own life and felt that my antagonism was a result of too many rules. He believed I would get through this stage on my own, and tried to give me the space to do just that, sure that what I was lacking was freedom and respect. He reacted to my outbursts with raised eyebrows and this made him an unsatisfying sparring partner. As a result, he saw the turbulent side of my personality far less than my mother, who provoked my rage with her constrictive measures. He remained stoic, believing me to be the same as I had always been, with the world at my fingertips.

My mother was full of reproach. She knew that I, the sinner with the black heart, had manipulated my father by donning a sheepskin over my dark wolf's coat. She tried to warn my father, who responded with the slightest roll of the eyes. My mother clenched her jaw and waited for the opportunity to prove that I was, in fact, in need of a shorter leash and a good dose of Scripture.

I presented her with that opportunity myself. What my parents didn't know was that I was as weary of my erratic behavior as everybody else. I hated continuously living in fear and paranoia. On many levels, I understood my mother's need to contain me, to take away everything I loved until I proved deserving. I was not as confident in the success of this procedure as my mother, however. Unlike my parents, I knew why I had become an unstable person, and I knew I would never be the same. I hated myself for it. I wanted out: out of my house, out of my family, until I could figure out a way to be whole. There was only one place I thought someone like me belonged – the psychiatric ward.

I devised a plan that would accomplish this. I looked for something that would make a point, something with shock value, something dangerous and something I could control in case I changed my mind. One day it came to me: I was going to burn my room to the ground.

Early on Sunday morning, I put on my church clothes. I stacked my homework on my dresser in a neat little pile, with my assigned English reading, *The Giver,* on the top. I lit a match, hovering over the book to give myself last-minute pause. Then I dropped it. I watched the flames curl the edges of the book and then die out. It was a little disappointing, and it made me uncertain. How many matches was I willing to light?

My father called me to the front door for church, and I had no choice but to leave my discouraging pile of slightly burned paper where it was.

I had been so wrapped up in my own somber plans that I had forgotten that this particular Sunday was my younger sister's Baptism. We arrived at church and my delighted father invited any and all who were hungry to come to our home for a celebratory lunch.

This complicated my plans, which had declined from starting fires to a serious discussion in which I would request politely to be taken to a therapist after admitting to attempted pyrotechnics.

The afternoon progressed, and we drove home with no less than twenty guests in tow, many of whom entered our house and remarked of the faint aroma of burnt cookies. This alarmed my father, who suspected a clogged vent or a candle left burning, and he went in search of the source. He emerged from my room holding the partially charred book in his hands, his face a mixture of unbelief and confusion.

Our guests gasped.

"This is an act of God!" said one.

"I have always had reservations about that book," said another, who had encouraged me to throw my copy of *The Secret Garden* into the flames at our last church Book Burning event.

"What does this mean?" they all wondered, pondering the significance of such a display of God's power on this, the holy day of a Baptism. I myself offered no explanation, but I began to doubt that it was me who needed psychiatric help.

My mother also remained silent. While my church didn't oppose book burning, my mother did. If God was going to go lighting things on fire, she was sure it wouldn't be an award winning novel. Not in her house. She looked at me with renewed suspicion.

When I was at school the next day, she entered my bedroom and combed through my desk, my books, my rows of porcelain dolls, until she found what she was looking for.

My journal.

CHAPTER SEVEN

What To Tell Your Therapist

Sex education was a tenuous concept at my Christian school. Parents and teachers alike assumed that we would all grow up to learn through experience, an experience we would not have until our wedding night with our equally inexperienced spouses. Any discussion attempted by curious students was buffered with a cheerful reminder that premarital sex was a sin, as was thinking about premarital sex, and did we want to pay for promiscuous thoughts with eternal damnation? Surely not. Turning to my only available resources, I relied on my limited experience with Hollywood movies to fill in the blanks.

Pregnancy was another matter. I grew up holding my mother's hand as we picketed abortion clinics, each of us grasping our handmade signs and tearfully praying for unborn children everywhere. By the time I was in middle school, I could accurately report every medical detail of any given trimester. How a baby got *in* there, and how a baby got *out* were murky details.

When I finally chose to disclose my weighty secret of my language teacher to a school friend, the specifics of what happened were never reviewed. What she wanted to know was, had my clothes been taken off? More or less. Had his clothes been taken off? More or less. Did we kiss? Yes.

We thought about this and came to an irrefutable and undeniable conclusion. I was pregnant.

I took this news in stride. I had been prepared for this moment, it seemed. I had a script. I'd witnessed my mother begging the young unwed women on their way to get abortions to give their little miracles up for adoption. Obviously, I would have my baby and then adopt him or her out to a good Christian couple who would no doubt praise God for the gift I had provided them with. It would make the whole mess beautiful and meaningful.

This is exactly what I wrote in my journal. In between my rambling teenage angst and a few top-ten music lists, I wrote about my conflicting feelings about giving birth to a child who was the result of such a negative experience. When my mother read this, she brought it to my father as evidence, but he was so scandalized by my mother's invasive detective work that he refused to even open up my journal, and he instructed her not to confront me regarding anything she may have read.

As it turned out, she was not the only concerned mother. My friend from school had told her mother, who told the school principal, who told my parents, who immediately took me to the doctor's office for a pregnancy test. When the results came back negative, and a physical exam further proved that I was not expecting a child, I was relieved. For the first time in a long time, something had turned out just the way it should.

My happiness made my mother more suspicious. She added lying about a pregnancy to the list of my proposed offences, and used the only method at her disposal for uncovering the truth – the court system.

I was taken to the police station, where I gave a rather shaky testimony to two frustrated police officers. They asked questions I didn't know the answer to, and alluded to things in a way that made me feel like a liar even when I was saying all I knew. I began to stutter and sob, and with more than a few exaggerated sighs they ended the interrogation and I signed where they told me to, silently doubting the process and wondering if justice was a real thing, or just a made-up adult word.

Despite my incomplete statement, the charges went ahead and the response in our Christian community was overwhelming. There were questions about what *actually* happened, and outright disbelief. The worst came from Team Perpetrator. He denied it, his wife believed him, and their friends supported them in that. They just could not believe that I would try to destroy such an amazing couple, and believed that my testimony was a direct attack from Satan. The fact that I had taken it so far, that my harrowing untruths were now to be heard before a court of law, had them worried about my mental health. Had I looked into deliverance? There was a travelling exorcist in town who dealt with possessed teenagers *just like me.*

As betrayed as I felt, not all reactions were so unpleasant. My schoolmates and teachers were as supportive as they knew how to be, and my father, who had been at his wits' end ever since the book burning incident, considered all my ill-conduct forgiven, and not one word was ever spoken about it again by him. I was awkward with my father at first. He now knew what I had tried so hard to keep hidden, and I knew his friends and fellow missionaries were shocked by what they viewed as lies. But over time I saw that our relationship would not be affected by others' opinions on the event, as he never considered any version but mine.

The custodians of order at our local courthouse saw things from a more progressive point of view. They were unencumbered by religious views that said sexual abuse was unthinkable, especially at a Bible Study and absolutely not during worship. But they wanted physical proof, and the time span between the incident and the date reported made finding evidence impossible. I was advised that without anything concrete, the best I could hope for would be a report, which would bolster the testimony of anyone else he tried to assault if he ever tried to assault anyone.

It was at this point that my mother brought forth my journal, which was photocopied beginning to end and handed out to legal teams. I was unaware of this until I was summoned to a private meeting with the Crown, where she reviewed my journal page-by-page and, to clarify things, asked me questions such as "Are you dating boys at school? Do you want to have a baby? Do you feel attracted to the opposite sex?" She probed for a narrative, a description of who I was and what I had felt, and it gutted me. I spent the duration of that meeting sobbing into my sweatshirt.

My mother wanted me to take the stand, but everyone else had reservations. I was emotional and withdrawn, which made for an unsuitable courtroom disposition. My mother tried to plead with me, but I saw her as a traitor for bringing my journal to the table, for even reading it in the first place, and I would not listen to a word she said. The court date was set, and I would not be required to speak.

The court date came, but nobody arrived to refute my charges. Taking this as an admission of guilt, a restraining order was drawn up and I was awarded the option of government-funded therapy. I gratefully accepted. Therapy was exactly what I wanted, what I had been wanting for some time.

That night, alone in my room, I cried grateful tears, relieved that it was over for good and that my sanity was going to be restored by the competent hands of professionals.

Therapy was to take place for the duration of one year, and my mother went on the hunt for the most trustworthy Christian counselor she could find. Trustworthy, meaning she could count on her not to steer me in the direction of secular psychology. I was hoping for a kindred spirit, someone who could guide me through emotional upheaval and my impending identity crisis. I wanted to talk about how I wasn't sure my parents' religion matched the beliefs I was forming about the world. I wanted to talk about how I needed space, but not too much space, and freedom, but not too much freedom. I wanted to talk about how I was scared and sad and lonely and full of fear and anger, and how I felt like this made me different than my peers, different in a sad, broken way.

I wanted to say all these things, but I didn't, because my therapist was a Christian, which I resented. I was untrusting and cautious, but despite this she was very sincere in her desire to help me.

She took notes while I colored pictures and talked about my mother, how I abhorred her rules, her constant badgering about church and her fondness for verbal grammatical accuracy. "As if" was not a sentence, it was disrespectful jargon. So was "no way" and "buzz off," and my personal favorite, "Oh my word." I couldn't handle it, I told my therapist. My mom wants me to speak in complete sentences and go to Youth Group every single day of my life.

Even though I never spoke about abuse, over time, I learned a few things. I learned that listening to yourself was a big deal. I learned that emotions were not a problem, that beneath the tears there was always a deeper truth, and that turning off meant not hearing what your body and mind were trying to say. My therapist taught me that shame and guilt were not the same as fear and anger, that the first two came from listening to and believing others, and the second two came from listening to yourself. She taught me to analyze, to abandon my favorite words, "Always" and "Never" and to choose carefully whose opinions I cared for.

This was gold. I practiced these new skills at home, at church, and at school, and one day I realized something. I was surrounded by people with the same perspective, people who didn't accept diversity of opinions. I began to investigate other methods of thinking. Instead of just repeating words I'd heard my parents say, I began to question what they meant. I wasn't being argumentative, at least not all of the time. I was using a newly discovered ability to think critically about events that were transpiring before my eyes. And what I saw was problematic.

CHAPTER EIGHT

Revival In The Land

It was around this time that our conservative church became a *charismatic* conservative church. Our congregation was whacked on the head with the Holy Spirit. Our church leaders embraced the practices of laying-on of hands, prophecy, speaking in tongues, and being "slain in the Spirit". It was not uncommon for our Pastor to laugh for fifteen or twenty minutes solid while preaching, so joyous was he to be filled with the Holy Spirit. Nobody minded, because they too were laughing, or rocking back and forth with outstretched hands, or standing up on chairs to speak the word of God while the Pastor was clearly enjoying His company on stage.

All who felt the call of the Lord were encouraged to speak out, coherently or otherwise, standing or sitting or laying down in the middle of the aisle to shout. While it may have been voluntary at first, soon it became a widely supported theory that only true Christians had the Gifts of the Spirit. Those who were skeptical or unwilling were obviously lacking in faith and there was no room in our church for that kind of poison.

I had received a gift myself. My church had unknowingly provided the perfect opportunity for me to put my new critical thinking skills to the test. I went undercover. When the Pastor asked those with unaddressed sin in their hearts to come to the front for prayer, I was the first in line. Oh, they were thrilled. The prodigal daughter had seen the light.

To support me in receiving the Holy Spirit, two Elders of our congregation surrounded me while the Pastor prayed into the microphone for my repentant soul. I was lowered ever closer to the floor until I was on the ground head to toe. *Act natural,* I told myself, as I closed my eyes. I knew from previous observations that I would be expected to be laying there at the feet of God for at least half an hour. I waited for the Holy Ghost to show up and fill my soul, but as I predicted, nothing happened. I stuck it out as long as I could, until someone in the front row caught me opening one eye to look around. I got up, stretched, and said to the person laying down to my right, "I have been so *blessed*!" She didn't open her eyes.

As this revival continued, I began making a list of questions. Why is it that women could pray, bake, sew, and clean, but not stand at the pulpit and preach? Why did we spend so much time memorizing minute details of the Bible, such as the great commandment No Jeans On Sunday, and yet fail to remember the really important ones, such as Love Your Neighbor? Why did we need to change everyone who walked through the door, instead of accepting them for who they were? I suspected that I knew the answer.

By the time I sat my parents down to inform them of my decision, it had already been done. I looked into their eyes and unveiled the new me. I was not a Christian any longer. The good news, though, was that I was exactly the same. I just wouldn't be going to church.

Religion wasn't a way to make someone better, I revealed to my parents, it was a way to control people. Nobody could tell me who I needed to be.

My father laughed, thinking that surely this was a joke. My mother, having known all along that I was a fraudulent child of God, pertly nodded her head. When my father left the room, she asked me the only question she could ask.

"Why?"

And though I'd learned to think for myself, I hadn't learned to be nice about it, so I said the only thing I could say.

"All your church friends are crazy."

Before renouncing my faith, I had made a battle plan. I was prepared for my parents' predictably adverse reactions. My plan was to dig in my heels and howl. My mother, who had predicted my exit from Christianity, adopted a similar tactic. My combative nature rose to the challenge, and I waited for the opportunity to fight.

Unfortunately, my mother was as determined to take me to church as I was to avoid it. I was going, and whether I wanted to or not I was going to hear God's message. I railed against her, pulling every dirty trick out of my sleeve, but come Sunday morning I would be packed into the minivan with the rest of my family and we would go to church.

There, my war cry against religion only grew louder. "You can't make me do anything!" I would tell anyone who would listen, and some who weren't listening at all. I publicly declared that I cared little about the growing opinion of me as a rebel and a lunatic, but when people responded to me as such, I would spit venom. I accused people of hypocrisy and informed them, with my finger in their face, that Jesus was all about love. Weren't they bound by their beliefs, required to respond to my every jab with graciousness and humility? I would be the one to put them to that test.

It was not long before all my personal vendettas became wrapped up in one person. My mother.

She embodied everything that was wrong with Christians everywhere. Ever true to my cause, I set about to publicly humiliate her, not only to teach her a lesson, but to set an example for my friends, who I felt were also suffering under the burden of being raised in Christian families.

One day she'd had enough, and tearfully delegated the task of raising me to my father, who had watched this develop and wisely chose a different approach.

As my lone parent left standing, he made some small concessions, which meant a great deal to me after the long and arduous battle with my mother. I would still be required to go to church, but I could wear what I wanted, even jeans. I could go to my friends' houses and listen to music, even if it was the Spice Girls. In solidarity, he would bob his head to top-ten pop songs as he drove me to various sleepovers, where he would drop me off with a smile and a wave, not once asking if he could stay to supervise.

I felt like the noose had been loosened, and I responded by scaling down my drastic attempts to bring the church and my parents to their knees. Now that there was nobody to stop me, I threw myself into the world of magazines, makeup, and movies. When my mother expressed concern over my new obsession with beauty products and famous actors, my father responded by grabbing the car keys and offering me a ride to the movie theatre.

While I was busy painting my nails and putting up *Titanic* posters, my father was working hard to finish his degree. When he graduated with a Masters in Divinity, he was hired as a Chaplain and liaison for Kosovo refugees, his job to provide these war-worn peoples with both life-giving bread and the Bread of Life.

This new chapter in my father's career meant that we had to move to the inner city. I left behind the best friends I had known in childhood. I said goodbye to the tree-lined cul-de-sac and unpacked in a new bedroom overlooking a busy street and a bus stop. I felt like I was starting over just when I'd gotten sure footing in my personal life.

If I had any reservations about our new neighborhood, they were muted by the momentous occasion of getting my license. Not only could I now drive, but my father purchased a junk heap of scrap metal that the auctioneer had the nerve to call a vehicle, my new great love. I spray-painted my car bright blue and drove it everywhere, the wind in my hair and nothing but a cracked vinyl seat to keep me company.

Our new home brought a breath of fresh air into the relationship between my father and I. He chose to accept my enmity against the church, and he informed me that if I wanted to spend Sunday mornings in bed instead of sulking in the back of a church service, that was alright with him. Not only that, but if I didn't want to start the new school year in the same religious private school as my sisters, he would happily oblige, as long as I found a suitable alternative and maintained my grades.

I had been dreaming of public school, but after all my years of religious education, I was uneasy and afraid to wade into the heathen waters. High school terrified me, and public high school all the more. I was intimidated by my non-Christian peers, who did as they pleased without the demon of regret and remorse that seemed to follow me everywhere. Admitting this felt like defeat, so I explored other options, and discovered to my relief that high school could be completed by correspondence.

I threw myself into my school work, completing a year's worth of work in less than two months. By then, two months of isolation had left me desperate for conversation and money for my car, so I decided that instead of going ahead to the next year and graduating early, I would work full-time and begin school again in September.

I was hired at a furniture factory staining lumber. As an underage, friendless, high school student, I was happy to scrub and lacquer wood all day long. With arms wide open, I accepted the daily grind of what I considered to be normal life – working, eating, sleeping, and working some more.

Perhaps it was the onslaught of chemicals I was breathing in on a daily basis, but my morale soon began to plummet. I was restless once more, disappointed with the satisfaction I had yet to find in the routine of working and living. The pointlessness of it all weighed down on me, choking me in a necklace of despair. I searched for meaning and came up empty-handed.

I knew that I lacked passion, some internal mechanism that gave meaning to ordinary tasks. I explained this dilemma to my father, who looked at me with the knowing eyes of a kindred spirit and pointed me in the direction of academia, sure that education was a path that would lead me to my purpose. I agreed. It was so obvious. Knowledge was the only thing worth striving towards.

I was going to finish high school as quickly as possible, immediately departing for a foreign university. I replaced the posters on my wall with extensive five and ten-year plans, which included four years at Stanford, where they would be lucky enough to have a student such as myself in attendance.

Once my outstanding academic life had been extolled as a goal which other, inferior students should strive towards, I would graciously turn down a full scholarship and would then complete a Masters degree at Oxford, after which I would become a world-renowned journalist who traveled the globe uncovering sensational truths.

It was fool-proof, except for the part where I was not actually going to school. I'd seen more than my fair share of *Gilmore Girls* and I knew that I needed to graduate from a real high school, not one where I mailed in my homework. A school with uniforms. A school with the word "academy" in it.

As it happened, my sisters went to a school such as this, a school that prided themselves on academic excellence and strength of character. The fact that it was a religious institution was a minor detail, a small price to pay for the sake of my grandiose plans. With the student handbook in my arms, I presented my idea to my father, who expressed resistance.

"You just spent a year with a fair amount of freedom," my father cautioned, "are you ready to spend the next year with your peers, abiding by rules you may not agree with and following a religion you don't want to be a part of?"

Undeterred by his logic, I reminded him that rules were my new thing. Education was my top priority. If I wanted to positively impact society, I had to make sacrifices along the way.

He put up both hands in a gesture of assent, and without reading a word, I signed a Statement of Faith and measured myself for my new uniform.

This grand school of virtue, built upon the twin foundations of legalism and pretentious spirituality, accepted my enrolment on one condition. I would be required to dye my newly bleached hair a more natural shade, preferably the same shade God had blessed me with before I'd been vain enough to alter it.

Not knowing how to abandon a bad idea before seeing it through to its disastrous end, I agreed, and the next day I drove into the parking lot starched, collared, and brunette.

CHAPTER NINE

Teacher Of The Year

I walked through the wide glass doors of the school full of expectations. I'd been promised, as per the student handbook, an education that would instill excellence of character. I assumed this would be taught in class, maybe with step-by-step instructions and a few bonus reading materials. I wanted information. I wanted lists and suggestions. I wanted an approach that would allow me to take advice or leave it based on what applied to me personally.

I soon realized that the mantra of "thinking for yourself" was on par with renouncing one's faith. I was back in familiar territory. Of course I believed in God, I told my slack-jawed teachers. I just didn't like Christians, the church, militant spirituality, performance-based ideology, people who judged, hypocrites, and those in leadership who misused their positions of power to brainwash others, but hadn't we all gotten tired of those types of people?

No. They had not. Furthermore, and much to my disappointment, this school believed that excellence was not something to strive towards as much as it was a strict standard by which you could measure every moment of your waking hours. True excellence could only be found by submission to God and the ever-growing list of school rules.

Arriving to class late, failing to button up the top button of your stiff collar, and low test scores were signs of a sinful and wayward heart. I discovered the seriousness with which they abided by rules by not abiding by them, and subsequently spending every morning of my first week in the principal's office. I was still adjusting to the drastic changes, and trying to figure out how to maneuver within the confines of a box I had willingly jumped into, when I made the grievous mistake of wearing closed-toed Birkenstock sandals over my heavy knee-high socks.

Luckily, this mistake was brought to my attention before I'd had the chance to wander the halls and lead other students astray with my inappropriate footwear.

As had become my morning routine, I was directed to the principal's office, where I was told that sandals were for walking on the beach with my husband, and I would not be permitted to drive home to find replacement shoes. They didn't approve of their senior students driving off campus and they saw no reason a female student should have a license or a car. No other girls in my senior class had their license, and why should they? They had fathers.

My own father was called, and he left work to bring me a new pair of shoes. Irritated by what he considered to be a fashion problem, he arrived at the school with a pair of shoes from the donation box for refugees.

"Just wear the right shoes!" he said when I gave him an ungrateful stare, and we went our separate ways with exasperated sighs.

The first month of my senior year progressed. In English class, we were studying *Macbeth*, and I was given photocopies of the play where line after line of questionable literature had been inked out with the wide stroke of a marker. I had studied *Macbeth* already and managed to survive it, and when I dared to ask why we couldn't have actual copies, I was told that dubious textbooks such as that were no longer handed out, since several parents in previous years had objected to the dark and secular writings of William Shakespeare.

Near the end of fall, a new teacher took me aside and encouraged me to join a mentorship program, which did not sound absurd in a school that valued discipleship. She talked to me about the fear one might have if they were on the cusp of something great but hesitant to take the big leap over the proverbial line in the sand. I *did* feel fear, but I also wanted a mentor, someone who could write me reference letters for my college applications. She told me that she was the one, placed in my life by divine powers, to keep me accountable to my progress, that she would neither judge me nor give up on me, even though she knew I loosened my tie when I thought nobody was watching.

Our mentorship program seemed promising at first. Everything I said was hilarious, every report I did outstanding. I was so funny, so smart, so perfect in every way. I had never had a relationship with a woman, especially one in authority, which had been so affectionate and encouraging. I was starved for the level of attention that she was giving me, and I responded by following her around and mimicking her out-of-school attire, a wardrobe which consisted mainly of hockey jerseys. When I cut my own long hair short like hers, she developed a habit of running her hand down the back of my head and at the bottom, flipping her hand up in the same direction that my hair curled.

I was aware that this type of relationship was unusual between a teacher and a student, but I could say nothing against someone who so obviously loved me. My need for her was greater than any instinct to flee from her. We began to meet after school at her apartment, or at the hockey rink after her practices, or at the beach near her house. My mother became suspicious, but when she brought her concerns to me I lashed out at her. Not knowing what to do, she asked the school to suspend the mentorship program.

My mentor knew just what to do. Nobody was going to tell her who she could and could not mentor. After all, she had sacrificed to spend time with me. The least I could do was return the favor. From now on, we would only meet at night and I was to tell my parents I was working at a new job in a coffee shop.

I couldn't believe my mentor was so amazing. She was right, nobody could tell us what to do. Everyone always wanted to control me.

Well, I would show them. I would meet with anyone I wanted any time I wanted, as long as it was dark and nobody knew.

I told my parents how busy I was with homework and my job. I was never going to be home, I warned them. This lie was believable until I was invited to a birthday party and had to ask for money to buy a gift.

"Why don't you have money if you've been working so much?" my mother wanted to know.

I rolled my eyes and stormed off, and to avoid offering an explanation, I spent my last twenty dollars on a present.

I was getting ready for the party when I got a message from my mentor. She wanted to know if I could come over tonight, right now. I reminded her that I was on my way to a birthday party, which she knew because my friend was also her student and we had talked about it already.

Are any of these people really your friends? she wrote, *And let me guess... you got her lotion and body spray. So original.*

It was true.

I had bought a bath kit from The Body Shop. It had seemed like an okay present, but once I thought about it, I wasn't sure. Ugh. I should have known it was the worst present ever. I couldn't show up to the party with this in my hands, the gift that said "I bought this on sale at the mall."

I took the cellophane-wrapped gift of shame and walked out the front door, saying goodbye to my parents and telling them I would be back late. Then I drove towards the beach, heeding the call of my mentor.

She opened her apartment door and greeted me with a long hug. She was so excited – a new Michael Jackson cd had just come out and she couldn't wait for me to hear it. She made us tea with brandy and turned the music up. When I drank straight to the bottom, she motioned me to the couch. I sat beside her and she leaned close to my face, pointing to her eye.

"Do you see this small speck of brown?" she said. I nodded yes, and she continued, "They say the eyes are the window to the soul. You are in my soul."

It may have been the brandy, but I started giggling. It was so funny, I'd finally found a friend and here I was, planning to leave after graduation. Oh, life. So ironic. I couldn't stop laughing. I tried to explain, but instead of talking I lit a cigarette. I was in such a good mood that I didn't know I had been excused until I found myself being walked back to my car.

"I don't know where to go," I told my mentor. "It's not fair. I'm supposed to be at a party, I can't go home!" But I was talking to nobody. She had already gone inside.

I sat in my car with nothing to do but chain-smoke and apply vanilla-scented body lotion until I fell asleep.

The next day, I passed my mentor in an empty school hallway. I waved hello, but instead of returning the greeting she grabbed me by my sweater and pushed me up against the wall.

"If you ever tell anyone about us, you're dead." she growled. She let go of my clothes then shoulder-checked me as she walked away.

Insecurity and confusion, mixed with a bit of anger, boiled up inside of me. I'd woken up in a cold car with a pounding headache, all for the sake of mentorship, and this is how I got treated? For the first time, I started to think maybe my mentor wasn't as great as she'd told me she was. I narrowed my eyes and followed her, thinking I was going to demand an apology.

She ignored me when I called her name. She ignored me when I raised my hand in class. She ignored me when I tried to make eye contact. She acted as though she had never noticed me at all.

I was hurt.

I didn't know what I had done wrong and I didn't know how to say sorry. So I stopped showing up for our mentorship dates. In class, I turned my back to her and didn't do my homework. I excused myself to the washroom and wouldn't return until hours later. I wanted an explanation, but I couldn't bring myself to ask now that I was refusing to speak to her. *It's okay*, I thought. *I can wait.*

She responded to my passive-aggressive actions by telling other staff members how I was an alcoholic. How I'd found her address and showed up at her house unannounced. How she wished she'd never agreed to be my mentor, but I'd begged her and I was so unstable she felt compelled to help me.

I was angry. I saw a bully, someone who had tripped me up and then laughed as I fell. The school saw the teacher of the year, a colleague who had done her best to help a struggling student. I didn't want to defend myself to these stupid teachers. I didn't care what they thought about me. I didn't care about my stupid classmates or the stupid school, I just wanted to graduate and get the hell out of there What none of us knew was that my mentor was a pedophile who was destined to serve a jail sentence for having sex with a young girl from a hockey team she coached, and that their relationship would start in the same way our relationship had. But without this knowledge, I didn't feel as if I had dodged a bullet. I felt like I had been hit by one.

I tried to focus on school work, but a part of me kept looking for a fight. When a guest-speaker, a self-proclaimed prophet, was invited to speak at a school-wide assembly, I took a seat, ready to raise a cynical eyebrow and a few objections. He stood at the podium and described the account of a man who claimed to have gone to the pit of hell and returned to write a book about his other-world experience. On and on the prophet went, and at the end of the hour he invited anyone from the wide-eyed audience to come speak to him afterwards.

Great, I thought. *I've been* asked *to speak my mind.*

I walked through a sea of sideways glances to the front row, where I respectfully accused this man of fear-mongering and using skewed theology and fictional accounts to manipulate impressionable young minds. He responded as well as could be expected: by calling me Jezebel and screaming "I will not cast my pearls before swine!" while the worship team softly played music behind him.

It became obvious that I was not a good candidate for this particular brand of education. By springtime, I was in the principal's office for the last time. He sat behind his mahogany desk, fingers tapping the smooth surface, and told me that the poison in my heart was creating a toxic atmosphere for those around me, and that he needed to protect the school from influences such as myself.

"I think we both know your time here is up," he said, and the meeting was over.

It was true, my time there was up. I felt like we had, for the first time, seen things eye-to-eye. I'd been worn down by the constant friction and was relieved to say goodbye to my final year of school. To my father, my relief seemed a lot like insanity.

"I'm done with this stage of my life!" I told him. But in truth, I wasn't done. I was a few credits short of my high school diploma. My father, angry at me for being expelled, demanded that I go back to apologize and finish the year.

I refused. What ensued was my first-ever, no-holds-barred fight with my father, during which I told him, a man who had just toiled long hours to complete his Masters degree, that I would not be defined by a piece of paper, that I would not bow down to the god of education, that a high school diploma held no significance and that returning to that school was beneath me.

After a long stalemate, where neither of us relented or apologized, I packed my bags and ran away to the peaceful mountain town of Banff, where I spent my days working as a maid for a hotel, occasionally smoking marijuana and living what turned out to be a fairly normal, although short-lived, life.

"We are all just beginners here,

and we shall all die beginners."

Elizabeth Gilbert, *Big Magic: Creative Living Beyond Fear*

CHAPTER TEN

Toe The Line

My time in the Rocky Mountains was not to be. My father informed me, in a series of curt emails, that I was to return home or he would be forced to file a missing persons report since I refused to tell him of my whereabouts. I chose to call his bluff, and a week later the police tracked me to my work, where my confused employer, along with the policemen, encouraged me to return home.

I purchased a bus ticket and solemnly boarded the Greyhound for the long ride back to Vancouver. I arrived at my parents' house just before my birthday, and although the relationship with my father remained strained, he welcomed me back.

In my brief absence, my mother had turned my bedroom into a library. I was offered the couch and a clean set of bed sheets, which I accepted with a thin smile. Returning had been a mistake. My mother was hoping I wouldn't stay long and my sisters seemed unsure of me, like strangers wary of someone who might be dangerous. My father noticed my unease, and to encourage me not to run away again, he secured me a full-time job as a receptionist for his friend.

I didn't know then that I struggled with anxiety and depression. I didn't know how to find environments that were good for me. I just knew that I felt uncomfortable at my parents' house, and didn't know where I should be going or what else I should be doing. I was looking for a road to turn down, one that would take me away, and sometimes the wrong path is unveiled at the right time. On a beautiful summer evening, I ran into a friend from my Christian high school. He, too, had left school early. After it was discovered that his dreams of marriage included a husband, not a wife, he had been gifted an early diploma and a swift exit.

While I had been in the mountains cleaning hotel rooms, he had gone to Mexico where he discovered, among other things, crystal methamphetamine. I had never heard of this before, but to hear him describe it, this wonder drug had improved his health, his love life, and his mental stability. Looking at him, it was easy to believe. He was trim, manicured, and more self-confident than he had been in high school.

We exchanged numbers and parted ways. When my nineteenth birthday came around, this friend took me downtown Vancouver to my very first nightclub. I had been waiting for this day ever since I had seen *A Night At The Roxbury*, a movie which lead me to believe nightclubs were full of shiny disco balls and equally shiny miniskirts, a place where glamorous young individuals with a penchant for synchronized dance moves could party the night away, dancing free until the morning light.

It was not exactly as I'd imagined. After consuming shot after shot of complimentary birthday drinks, I could no longer hold back my disappointment. In a tearful confession, I told my friend that yes, I'd had fun, but where was the disco ball, the sequined outfits, the choreographed dancing? Had we gone to the wrong club?

He took me by the hand and gave me a smile. "Where you want to go is an after-hours club!" he announced.

With him leading the way, I stumbled and careened down the street, occasionally bumping into people and objects to whom I apologized profusely. I shouted to others walking the same direction as us, "We're on our way to the after-hours!" and offered warm invitations for them to join us.

After a few heartfelt conversations with lamp posts and passersby, we stopped at a dingy gate in the middle of a long brick wall, which opened to a flight of stairs that descended into the heart of an old building. I could hear the music already, the bass-heavy frenzy of techno. I closed my eyes, leaning against the gate and taking the moment in, and then down we went.

It was just as I had hoped, and it was full of men. It appeared that I was the only female in the room. This may have been awkward in another club, but not here. I was immediately surrounded by a group of beautiful boys who flocked towards me with outstretched arms, chattering about my hair and my interesting choice of accessories. It was too hard to have a conversation over the music, so in response I smiled and shrugged, and in unison they raised a hand to their hearts and smiled, like I was a puppy who had just performed a cute trick.

While I was entertaining my five new best friends, the friend who brought me disappeared around a corner and reappeared with a little bag in his hand. He steered me through a tangle of sweaty bodies to the bathroom, where we cordoned ourselves off in an unoccupied stall. He wiped the back of the toilet with his shirt and then dumped a small pile of white powder from the little bag.

Taking a credit card from his back pocket, he divided the pile into two even lines.

"Do you have any money?" he asked. I searched my purse and produced a five dollar bill. He was disgusted. "Do you have any idea how many hands touch low bills? Give me a twenty or a fifty."

I handed him a twenty dollar bill, which he rolled into a tight funnel. He leaned over and inhaled with the loudest sniff I had ever heard. "Happy Birthday!" he shouted as he placed the rolled-up bill into my hand.

I flicked it like a cigarette, the white residue on one end falling to the floor. I'd seen *Basketball Diaries.* I knew that heroin was bad, bad, bad. I watched him for signs of a heart attack. His eyes were glossy and his nose was running, but he appeared to be just fine.

"I never thought I'd do heroin," I told my friend, who was now dancing in the cramped stall.

"It's not heroin!" he laughed, twirling around with his arms straight up like a frantic ballerina. "It's crystal meth!"

I turned to face the white line on the back of the toilet seat.

This isn't going to kill you, I coached myself, leaning over in imitation of my friend. I put one end of the paper straw in my nostril, the other end on the back of the toilet where the white line was waiting for me, and took a big breath in.

This is going to kill me, I thought, my hands instinctively clamping on either side of my temple like a vice. I felt like I had poured gasoline up my nose and lit a match. The pain was such a surprise that I jerked backwards and stood against the stall door, hyperventilating and saying over and over "My brain! My brain!"

My friend wiggled over to me and pushed my hands down to my side. "Just wait until it kicks in, it won't hurt anymore then!" he said cheerfully, and then left me to go to the smoking room.

I went to the sink to drink water from my cupped hand. My friend had been telling the truth. A few excruciating minutes later, a euphoric energy began to course through my body. I could hear my heartbeat in my eardrum, which seemed to be beating in time with the music. When my friend returned to the bathroom to see what had become of me, he found me perched on the sink, legs crossed, cigarette in hand, merrily telling my entire life story to the men waiting in the bathroom lineup.

"My parents were missionaries!" I told two men who were making out against the wall. "Don't you think that's great?!"

Two days later, when I finally made it home, I fell asleep, dead to the world. When my mother woke me up to go to work, my first thought was, *I wonder if there's anything left in that little bag.*

It would be months before I realized it, but I had become an addict overnight.

Two weeks after my birthday, my friend who had brought me to the club became my roommate. I moved out of my parents house in the suburbs and into a two-room walk-up in downtown Vancouver. There, deep in the city and far from my parents, my drug use escalated. Soon I was calling in sick to work so that I could spend the entire day at home doing line after line. Then it was two days. Then it was three. Eventually, I was fired.

That was the first month of addiction.

Unemployment left my schedule wide open, and I filled my hours with drug binges and house parties with my new friends, all of whom I had met at an after-hours club. My days began and ended with drugs, blurring together and turning my body against me.

I was always hungry for something that my mind knew was a poison. I would talk about how much I hated drugs as I sat before a coffee table covered with them. I'd rant about how the high had taken over my life as I bent over to inhale. I'd cry over the monstrosity of my addiction, pacing the living room as the very drug I hated coursed through my veins.

I discovered that this was not good party conversation. The only way to end my ranting and raving was to ignore the source of my distress, so I silenced my subconscious by taking hallucinogens as well as maintaining my methamphetamine habit. Some days, I was high on six or seven drugs at once. My friends, themselves social drug users, slowly began to disappear. By the second month of my addiction, I had surpassed everyone I knew in my level of drug usage.

But instead of slowing down, I made new friends.

My high school roommate, one step ahead of me in the game, discovered a way to facilitate our increasing drug use. He became a dealer. Now, instead of wondering how to support our blossoming habits, our main concern became guarding the ridiculous amount of drugs being stored in our apartment.

We wondered what would happen if we were robbed, two teenagers straight out of private school, one gay, one a girl, and both of us high out of our minds.

Of course, there was a solution. We invited our supplier to move in with us. I vacated my room and found myself once more living on a couch, but this time it mattered less because I never slept anyway. I quickly became friends with the only other female, the supplier's girlfriend, who managed in a coarse and corrupt environment to create the feeling of an alliance, treating me like a younger sister and making sure I never went without.

While I spent my days doing other people's drugs, my high school roommate was building himself a small but profitable drug business. Coached by his new business partners, he developed a smooth, no-nonsense persona, becoming another person before my eyes. Animosity developed between us, and when I brought it up he coolly replied, "We don't like freeloaders."

He pointed out how this was no longer my apartment. How I needed to make money or get out. He had discussed this with some of his friends, he said, and they had all agreed that I should either work for him selling drugs or at an escort agency.

I was furious.

"I'd rather die than be a drug dealer!" I shouted for everyone in our building to hear.

"Then I think you know what to do." he said, with one eyebrow arched and a smug grin across his face.

CHAPTER ELEVEN

Hello, Mirror

I marched into the corner to sulk. I picked the peeling paint off the window frame and thought about my options. I was over my head in debt, unemployed, about to be evicted, and the friend who had held my hand and walked me down this road had turned his back on me. I thought about my life since I'd moved downtown, how I had shut my parents out. I knew how disappointed my father would be if he could see me now, curled up on a couch with only a pipe and a blowtorch to my name.

I saw my future unfold before my eyes – I saw my family, crushed to find that I was on a street corner selling my body for drugs. I saw in myself a weakness that was swiftly corroding my sanity and I doubted my ability to overcome it. I was certain that every step I took brought me closer to my tragic, sordid, harrowing death.

I hated the person I had become. I feared the person I would live to be. I knew that my addiction had opened a door that could not be walked through again. I knew that I would never be the same. I sat on the window sill and watched the low afternoon sun through the hazy city smog. I knew what I would do. Death was coming to find me, and I was going to help it along.

I found my high school roommate in his bedroom, measuring and weighing out little bags of various drugs. I sat down beside him and gave him my speech.

I apologized for being such a burden. I didn't know how or why he had put up with me or my partying. I promised him I would be a "freeloader" no longer. I was ready to work, I confessed. He had motivated me, I told him.

He nodded his head and I continued with my grand idea. If he would give me a bottle of GHB, I would bring it to the club that very night. It was Halloween, I reminded him. I was guaranteed to bring back money.

Encouraged by my change of heart, he handed me a water bottle full of GHB, a foul-tasting liquid, and warned me not to drink my own profits. "You owe me for this" he cautioned.

I took the bottle and left him with his work. Taking a deep breath, I drank as much as I could handle. Then, I took another breath and drank some more. I drank until I choked and sputtered. My heartbeat slowed and my eyes closed.

The last thought in my mind was, *Finally, I've done something right.*

And then I fell to the floor, unconscious.

The first time I opened my eyes, I was blinded by the bright light directly above my head. I turned, saw the numbers on the machine to the left of me, and fell unconscious once more.

The second time I opened my eyes, I saw a man in a white medical coat directing two others, who were placing warm blankets over my arms and chest. I wanted to ask where I was, but before the words were formed I was once again unconscious.

The third time I opened my eyes, I was alone. And I was hysterical. I realized for the first time that there were medical tubes protruding from every conceivable part of my body, and in a panic I began to pull them out. I fumbled with the wide tube that ran from my mouth down into my trachea, coughing up charcoal as I yanked it out. I ripped out my IV, kicked off my blankets and knocked my blood pressure monitor to the floor.

When several nurses rushed to hold me down, I tried to yell but I found I had no voice. I struggled silently as they strapped me to the bed by my hands and feet.

One might assume that being saved from death, even self-imposed death, would render one grateful, but I was furious. I raged inside myself as the nurses paged the doctor and whispered amongst themselves.

When the doctor arrived, he informed me that the hospital had called my parents, who were on their way, and that the next steps would be decided when they got there.

I found my voice.

"I'm discharging myself!" I whispered hoarsely to the horrified doctor, who informed me that this was against his medical advice and that if my intent truly was to leave the hospital, a consent form would have to be signed.

I narrowed my eyes into slits and made a rough barking sound, assuring him I was serious. He left, shaking his head, and returned with a clipboard and a backpack that one of my dear roommates had packed for me after calling the ambulance.

I was untied from my bed, and with my backpack in hand, I whispered "Bathroom" and was pointed down the hall. Away I shuffled, concerned eyes watching me all the way.

I locked myself in the bathroom and stood in front of the mirror, viewing this person who had come back to life with disdain. My hair was caked with vomit, my skin whiter than the hospital bed sheets and my pale mouth was lined black with charcoal. I had bruises all over my body and my gown was covered in blood from my desperate removal of the IV needle.

I looked the way I felt. Like a corpse.

In my backpack I found makeup, clothing, my wallet and a teddy bear that had been my childhood friend since my days on the ship. How it came to be there, I could not imagine, but the sight of this tiny comfort brought forth noiseless sobs and I sat shaking on the floor.

I had been such a failure. As a human being, as a daughter, and now, a failure in death as well. I'd wanted clean lines, a goodbye that would put an end to the pain I had caused, to the pain I lived with inside myself. I looked into the glass eyes of my childhood toy, eyes that had seen me grow and change and become this broken person.

I wanted to leave the hospital with nothing, to be nothing, taking none of my past with me. I washed my face, applied makeup, and left the bathroom with my belongings. I passed my hospital bed. It was untouched, exactly as it had been the moment I realized I was alive, the disarray a reflection of my terror of being in the world. I placed my teddy bear on the rumpled sheets then turned and walked out the hospital doors.

I returned to the apartment, burrowing in a pile of blankets to stare at the wall, where I stayed for several days. When I emerged, I put everything I owned into garbage bags. My clothes, pictures, posters, my entire wallet with all my identification. I carted my life outside to the dumpster and unceremoniously threw in one bag at a time. I kept only my makeup, a guard against the outside world.

My remaining friend, my adopted older sister, watched me as I struggled to live in this fog. The day I threw my things away, she cornered me and said "I know what you're doing and I'm not going to let you do it."

A taxi pulled up to the curb and she opened the door and shoved me inside, sliding in after me. We headed downtown, where I was introduced to a friend of hers, someone who operated what might best be described as a family business. It wasn't exactly legitimate, she warned, but she promised it would get me on my feet and I would never have to do anything I didn't want to do.

I nodded in agreement. I was in. Welcome to the family.

Encouraged by my new family, a crazed assortment of unlikely business associates that spanned a wide range of ages and backgrounds, I moved out of my first apartment and into a high-rise in the heart of Vancouver's financial district. I was given two jobs – shop with manufactured credit cards, and sort through stolen mail to assemble profiles. I was told when to sleep, when to do drugs, who to associate with, and when and where to work. I never made money or got to keep anything, as I always owed debts, and rent, and dues, but I could leave anytime and I was taken care of with food, a furnished apartment, and, always, my drug of choice.

I didn't want to leave. I liked not having to think for myself. I was following the path of others who were far more renegade than I, and I had yet to acquire an aptitude for self-preservation. I needed this family, they kept me safe and it was where I belonged.

The first time I ever got arrested, I had been out with my friend while he collected mail and we stopped for dinner in a hotel restaurant. We planned to pay with a stolen credit card, which we had not asked permission to use, but the rule was you had to eat at least once a day, so we agreed that it was okay. The card declined, and my friend introduced me to the concept of a dine-and-dash.

He was going to go have a cigarette, and I was to run. We would meet in the bushes across the street in five minutes. He crept out the side door and I waited at the table for the five-minute mark.

After five long minutes, during which I stuffed my face with the remaining food, I attempted to casually stroll out the front doors of the hotel lobby with a bread stick in my hand. I was stopped by our waitress, who flagged the hotel staff, who came to form a circle around me while I offered excuse after excuse while trying not to talk with my mouth full.

It slowly occurred to me that my plan was failing and in desperation, I catapulted myself through the circle of employees and tried to make a run for the door. I never made it. A loyal employee held me captive until the police arrived.

One of the things I had been repeatedly told since entering this life of crime was, should I ever be arrested, my sole responsibility was to keep my mouth shut tight. When the police arrived and asked me my name, I didn't answer. My address? I didn't answer.

Why couldn't I pay for my dinner? I didn't answer.

Left with no choice but to handcuff me, I was put into the back of a cruiser and driven to the holding cells in Vancouver, where I was told they couldn't process me without a name and address.

It's a trap! I told myself. *Stay strong!*

It was near dawn when I broke down. Bethany Granholm of No Fixed Address was given a court date and notice of a Promise-to-Appear, and was escorted through a large, metal, magnetically-locked door and deposited outside the law buildings, blinking in the beautiful morning sunlight.

As a reward for my first arrest, I was given a pack of cigarettes and the day off. I tried to keep moving, to be one step ahead of the moment where my mind would have a chance to think. I'd been told to fear jail, that the police were my enemy now. I ripped up the piece of paper with my court date on it and vowed never to let them get me again. They did.

I was picked up and released by the city police so many times that I got to know my arresting officers. They weren't rude, they were just doing their job. We were on opposing sides, yes, but we weren't enemies. I felt like we might get along if I were living a different life.

Some of the officers reminded me of my father, believing that I might one day be a better person if I just tried hard enough and found new friends. But I wouldn't try and I couldn't make new friends, because I was so busy fuelling my methamphetamine addiction and trying to escape from my sad and empty life.

CHAPTER TWELVE

Jailhouse Rules

Over time, I moved from the miasma of depression into a flagrant acceptance of my substance abuse. I defined myself by my addiction. I was proud of it. I became a shameless liar, a thief, someone who took pleasure in destruction and decay. I was living the lifestyle of the infamous and the insane, and I got my hands dirty and enjoyed it.

I started renting upscale apartments, giving fake names and bad checks. I had to move every month, but that was easy. I didn't own anything so all I had to do was pick up my purse and walk away. I felt bad for the people I was taking advantage of – bad because they were so stupid. *You should have known better than to trust me,* I told them in my head. *There's a lot worse than me in this world.* I told myself that I was doing them a favor by ripping them off, because next time they would know better.

The police were never far behind me. Sometimes I tried to give fake names to the arresting officers, but once they had arrested me a few times they stopped asking who I was and started giving me lectures about turning my life around.

"You don't know anything about me," I told them, but they did.

They could look me up on their little computers and see a long list of recent mistakes. On this date, Bethany Granholm pretended to be this person. On this date, Bethany Granholm pretended to be that person.

The only time I was ever myself was after the handcuffs went on. I didn't have anything with my actual name on it but a jail card. I only existed because of a criminal record.

During a short stint in a remand facility, I overheard two other inmates discussing a lucrative scheme that they had just been arrested for.

Armed with a pair of bolt cutters, they would enter leisure centers and gyms, and break the latches off the change room lockers. On a good day, they said to one another, they could walk out the front doors with as many as ten or fifteen wallets and car keys.

I took mental notes.

After being released early for good behavior, I invested in a pair of giant bolt cutters and a gym membership. I headed out in the early morning hours and signed into the gym, doing an obligatory five-minute run on the treadmill and bouncing once or twice on a yoga ball before heading to the locker room to carry out my plan.

I cut the lock on the locker closest to mine, exchanged my backpack for the one inside, and took off, streaking through the gym, breathlessly telling the stunned employees that I was late for work as I threw myself through the front doors.

I flagged down a taxi, but the gym employees, suspicious of my hasty departure, had checked the locker room, uncovered the broken lock and my backpack with the bolt cutters, and dutifully called the police. They were going to get me. The cab driver was notified via radio that his new customer was a wanted felon and he was instructed to drive me straight to a waiting police cruiser.

I was oblivious to the impending take-down. Getting comfortable in the back seat of the taxi, I rifled through the stolen backpack, where I found a wallet, car keys, and a clean pair of yoga pants.

What a score! I thought to myself as I slid off my jeans and tried on my new pair of pants. I didn't wear them for long.

The taxi door opened, and there were two police officers. I was read my rights and arrested, and to further implement justice, I was driven by the police back to the gym, where the unfortunate victim was waiting for her belongings to be returned. In response to a strong suggestion from my arresting officer, I handed the backpack to its rightful owner, who looked me in the eye and said, "Why would you do something like thaaa..... hey, are those my Lululemons?"

I'd expected the bolt cutter escapade to be just as fun as it was illegal, but nothing took the joy out of crime more than meeting my victim. And returning her belongings that I had just stolen. And changing out of her clothes as she watched with a mixture of pity and contempt. My lawless ways had reached a level of shamelessness that could not be justified.

I was helped back into the police cruiser and taken to my second home, jail. I was only scared of jail until I got there. The very first time I was remanded, I shivered in my handcuffs, imagining rows of iron bars and bare concrete, inmates who screamed and fought and banged their metal cups against their containment.

In reality, I found jail to be a lot like my Christian high school, and not only because the jail I seasonally lived in was a short distance away from my parents house. In fact, it was an even shorter distance away from the school. I could look out the Plexiglas window in my cell and see commuters, dog-walkers, and even trick-or-treaters in the fall. It reminded me of my old bedroom. Jail also ran on rules and a false sense of stability, which made it all the more familiar.

Upon entering the institution, you were given a shower, a uniform, and a medical intake, and if you talked right and acted wrong you could get the best meds. It took me a while to figure this out, so the first couple times I went to jail I was sober the whole time.

What I did learn quickly was that if you didn't fight or steal from other inmates, you could stay out of trouble and even make a few friends. My jail didn't have iron bars, either. It was divided into closed units, which had nice, one-bed rooms with magnetically-locking doors, vinyl-tiled floors, and even a toilet about four inches from your metal bed. It really wasn't too bad. The hardest part was learning to eat and sleep on a schedule again.

If you behaved you could sign up for programs, and I signed up for it all. I even signed up to get my GED, which turned out to be a good decision because, although the GED program was a joke and nobody did homework in jail, they served actual coffee, with creamer and sugar cubes. If you were sneaky you could go back to your unit with a bunch of sugar cubes rolled inconspicuously into your underwear, and sugar was gold. I traded sugar cubes for meals, favors, phone time and cigarettes when I could get them. What I didn't get was a diploma, but neither did anyone else and at the end of the semester we were all given a donut for trying.

I put my name down for work duty and was assigned laundry, which was one of the good jobs. This didn't last for long, though. I had just traded a bunch of sugar for three Vicodin and was caught more than once face-down on a pile of clothes, warm from the dryer, sound asleep and snoring.

"What else are you good at?" the guards wanted to know. I couldn't tell them, so I was taken off work duty and encouraged to find other pursuits.

I signed up for AA, which was not as fun as I had hoped. There were no donuts there, and there was coffee but they *watched* the sugar cubes. It was like they *knew* that nobody actually put fifteen sugars into a cup of coffee and suspected it was being pilfered and used as currency. I sat in my seat, sipping my sweet coffee and listening to the other women talk.

Around the table they would go, beginning with one sad woman and moving on to the next, until all who wanted to speak had been heard. I always remained silent. I felt like I didn't belong. These women all had a good reason to be drinking and using drugs, and here I was, a middle-class white girl, so broken on the inside when I'd been given a good life. They talked about wanting to get sober for their children, for their babies in foster care, or their grown children who were now coming to jail themselves. I had nothing to say, because I had no reason of my own to get sober. Who was I living for? Not even myself.

I left those meetings on a sugar high, but late at night when the door to my cell was locked and I was alone with my thoughts, I would wonder if my life would be different if I had someone to love. In jail, the structure and the organization didn't bother me. The inmates didn't hassle me, the guards never picked on me.

I was just lonely, and I knew that when I was released, the only thing that would make that loneliness disappear was a white line.

My parents, who never knew where I was or what I was doing when I wasn't in jail, saw my incarceration as a chance to visit me in a secure location, fairly certain that I would be there until my release date. They came every weekend, from the first time I called them from the jail until the day I got out. My mother would come one day, my father would come the next day, and I would chat about my amazing life behind bars from behind a partition, leaning up against the long clear wall that separated the inmates and their visitors from the outside world.

These visits meant a lot to me, although I tried to hide this with mundane conversation. My parents were the only link I had to my old life, and when I wasn't on drugs, it became clear to me that I didn't want to die an addict. The jail visits with my mom and dad were the only sane and rational conversation I had for years, and their continued presence assured me that they did still want me in their lives.

I had been in for over five months when Christmas time came around, and another inmate, who had become my friend after she accidentally punched me in the face during a hallway brawl, was teaching me how to make toffee balls with popcorn and caramel from the canteen. We sat around a table with several other inmates, singing and laughing, and it occurred to me that if I managed to stay sober, I might have a Christmas like this in real life.

You know your journey has come to a dead-end when jail seems like the happy place. When you start wondering how your street life can be just like your jailhouse life, something has to change.

Just as a scandalous life of crime jerked me from the precipice of suicide, so jail, in the same unconventional way, managed to take me from my addiction, and slowly but surely, I began to hope of a future. I rediscovered within myself the girl who believed in checklists and plans, and I made a New Life Survival Plan.

1. First, I needed a job.

2. Once I had saved enough money, I would move far away from Vancouver.

3. Then, I would finally get over my fear of long-term relationships and I would get myself a boyfriend.

4. Finally, we would get married and have kids.

I went easy on myself and decided I would be flexible with the order, as long as all these things managed to occur, and preferably within a short time frame to eliminate the possibility of relapse. I memorized my list and talked of nothing else. By the time I was released, anyone who had so much as passed me in the hallway knew that I was going clean up and go far.

The Mugshot on my Inmate Phone Card

CHAPTER THIRTEEN

Sandwiches And Coffee

My Christmas wish came true. I was released early for good behavior and was given probation just before the holidays. I said goodbye to my inmate friends with a hug, sure that I would never see them again. I'd finally developed the will to move beyond this life, and willpower was everything. I was going to follow the step-by-step plan, the one I had made for myself, and I was going to find my someone to love.

I moved back into my parents house and got to work on Step One, which was to get a job. I crafted my resume with that purpose in mind, eschewing honesty in favor of principle. The principle was, I needed to work, and I was going to be a good employee, so nobody should know what I had been up to these past few years.

I was hired at a coffee shop down the street from my parents' house, where I regularly served police and corrections officers on their way to work in the jail I had just been released from. I hid behind the espresso machine and hoped that real clothes and my new hair color would be enough to confuse customers who might recognize me from the jail, and sure enough I was never found out. Step One was complete.

I moved on to Step Two, but I didn't even have to save money to get my ticket out of Vancouver. To my amazement, my family had managed to live their lives without me. My father had filed for divorce and had joined the Canadian Military, and he was leaving my mother and moving to a remote Air Force base in Northern Canada.

The military base was part of a small Canadian town. Like many Canadian towns, it was best known for wide open spaces and ten-foot snow drifts. *Perfect!* I said to myself, and begged my father to take me along. He agreed that the change of scenery would be a new beginning for both of us.

I put everything I owned into a laundry basket, and with half of my family, travelled as far North as I have ever been. I settled in and began to look for work. There seemed to be two options in this quaint little town. One was the bar. Or, if you preferred nine-to-five employment, the liquor store. I tried to find a job that best suited my personality and my probation restrictions, but I was fired from my first job for dropping a bottle of wine, after which my options were limited.

My father, whose love has no bounds, saw an opportunity to remedy this when a local bulk store came up for sale. He paid far more than it was worth and appointed me Owner, Operator and Manager. My first order of business, I declared, would be to turn the run-down bins of spices and five-blend flours into a bustling coffee shop. Blinded by his hopes and dreams for me, my father opened a line of credit and waved goodbye as he left for basic training.

It took me less than two months to run the store to the ground. I spent all our resources renovating the building and marketing our new "sandwich and coffee shop". I invested in what I thought was sure to be the next big thing, Italian Sodas. I was astonished to find that nobody wanted to leave their homes in forty-below weather to buy flavored sodas with cute names and whipped cream toppings. Even my own grandparents, who had responded to my tearful request for accounting expertise and age-old wisdom by travelling North themselves, were reluctant to brave the snow for a sandwich and a coffee.

My father came home to a broken dream and an empty wallet. While he accepted my failure and the lingering debt with graciousness, I was not so composed. My self-worth was hanging by a thread.

I knew it was a terrible combination of my inadequacy and mismanagement that had caused the bulk store and sandwich shop to fail. I also knew that it would be my father who paid for my mistakes, quite literally.

Full of discouragement, I searched my soul, desperate to know if there was anything I could excel at, if there was a calling for which I had been placed on this earth. I tried to talk myself out of my oncoming depression, but the sad part of me made such valid points. I wasn't good at anything and I had no skills. My life was going to be one big failure after another. The only thing I could hope for was to not disappoint the people who loved me, or to disappoint them as little as possible.

I had no choice but to move on to Step Four. After the business failure, the idea of marriage and a family became obsessions. This dream was my last hope, and I was getting old, my maternal clock was ticking. I was in my mid-twenties, and teenagers everywhere were on their second or third pregnancy and here was I, with no baby to call my own.

It was so clear to me now. My entire life had been an introduction to parenting. All those hours babysitting, of caring for my younger sisters, my place as a woman of childbearing age, these pointed to my absolute purpose in life: motherhood. I finalized my plans for marriage and children, whichever came first. The only complication I could foresee was that the man I was casually dating wanted neither.

One fine summer afternoon, after a routine pap-smear with my doctor, I received a phone call.

"Don't be alarmed," I was told by the voice on the other end, "but your test results came back...abnormal. Your cells are changing rapidly, and we want to schedule a cone biopsy."

When is this "biopsy" I wanted to know, trying to remember what a biopsy was.

It was the next day, and I was not to be late.

There was nothing that frightened me more than knowing that I knew nothing, especially about what might be wrong with my own body. *It's all the drugs you took,* a voice inside me said, *you should have known something terrible was coming.*

I spent a sleepless night tossing and turning, imagining the worst, and arrived at the hospital the following morning for a medical procedure that did nothing to dispel my fears. I drove home with my hands clenching the steering wheel, trying not to panic or vomit, both of which happened despite my efforts.

I received another phone call forty-eight hours later.

I had cervical cancer, I was informed. But, the good news was that my doctor had scheduled a surgeon on short notice and I was already booked for surgery, which was to take place in a few short days.

I hung up the phone and called the one person I never knew I would need.

My mother.

She flew out to hold my hand and provide much needed female solidarity. I had given the news of my condition to my new boyfriend, who asked me what a cervix was, and my father, who politely asked if I could find my mother a hotel while she was visiting. I ignored them both.

The surgery went well and was successful, and with my mother by my side and painkillers in my system, the doctor outlined my recovery. I was going to heal wonderfully, he said, and I would be just great. Unfortunately, he was doubtful that I would ever have children. Even if I were to conceive, he said, it was likely that I would miscarry before I even realized I was pregnant. He patted my hand and walked away, leaving me in the recovery room to sweat out my crushing sorrow.

Just as the doctor said, I bounced back to optimal health. The only permanent damage had been to my hope for a future, which left a sickness that no surgeon could repair. I had believed myself redeemable if only I could fulfill the role predetermined by my gender. If I couldn't be a mother, then who was I but an ex-criminal and a struggling addict, and who would want me then? How could I ever repay my debt to society if I didn't have someone whose life I could make better?

My mother reminded me that I had brought this on myself. "Virgins don't get cervical cancer," she said, as she lamented that with my criminal record, I wouldn't be able to adopt, either. I would just have to live with the consequences of my actions and find another way to contribute to the world. "Have you thought of going into Missions overseas?" my mother wanted to know.

I was directionless. My new life plan had failed miserably. As usual, I was good at climbing high enough to fall hard. I was also good at running away.

I told my father that I was going back to Vancouver to go to University. Then I found all my old downtown friends, the ones who weren't in jail, on this new thing called Facebook. I made plans to go see them, just to say hello before I started school.

"Don't go!" said my father, and to avoid an argument, I loaded up the car while he was at work, left a note, and drove the long, winding road back to Vancouver, only stopping for red bull and gasoline.

A part of me did want to go to school, the part that hoped for a future self. But there was a part of me that feared my worst self, the part that doubted and discouraged me from progress.

Don't do things you know you can't do, my fear said to me, *it will just make you sad. You know you're an addict. An addict. Addict.*

Even the rational part of me agreed with my fear. I had no evidence that I would be able to succeed at anything. I believed that the long-term impact of my earlier life choices would never be undone, that all the things that had gone wrong in my life had permanently derailed me. My body was against me, my mind was against me, and I felt helpless.

I half-heartedly thought about signing up for pottery classes and zumba sessions instead of University, but I was sidetracked by a message from an old jail pen pal. When I first heard of him, he had been serving a prison sentence for killing a police dog, and before that, he'd been serving a prison sentence for a high-speed chase in a stolen car. I was in jail myself back then, and he was writing letters to another inmate.

"You have to read this mail – it's hilarious!" she told me. It was dirty jailhouse romance. I found out what jail he was in and responded to the letter myself, and we exchanged jail mail for a long time after that. We lost touch when I stopped getting arrested.

When I found him again, he had just been released and had discovered Facebook himself. He hadn't heard from me in a while, and wanted to know what happened. Was I not going to jail anymore? That was a bummer. He could only be friends with people who wrote interesting letters.

"Do you want to hang out?" I asked. "It would be nice to catch up with you in between jail terms. You know, to see you in real life."

We had our first date in his favorite place, the casino. He took out a little bag of methamphetamine and made lines on the back of his phone case, chivalrously holding it out for me to go first.

"Well, I shouldn't," I began, "I'm probably going to school soon."

"We both know you're not going to school," he replied, grinning from ear to ear. I agreed. We got high and spent all our money on the slot machines.

Later that evening, as I vomited onto the curb outside, he rubbed my back and tried to console me. "I'll just make more money and we can move in together!"

That idea sounded just as good as anything I had come up with earlier. I didn't know that he was living out of a stolen car, but by the time I figured it out, I didn't care.

"The truth is that falling hurts.

The dare is to keep being brave and

feel your way back up."

Brené Brown, *Rising Strong*

CHAPTER FOURTEEN

Hey, Girl

I tried my hardest to be a functioning addict. I kind of liked sleeping in a bed, I told my new boyfriend. So we moved out of the stolen Audi and in with his mother. I made myself another resume, one with more lies, and got hired at the diner down the street. I knew I was walking a fine line, a difficult line. I had discovered that my boyfriend was demanding and possessive. I knew that I might one day end up doing something illegal to fund my revived addiction. I knew that I couldn't stay there, in that apartment with his mother, who did more drugs than both of us combined.

He knew that I wavered in my loyalty to him, that I might one day wake up and decide to do better, and it caused him to be controlling. He didn't want me to talk to anyone or do drugs with anyone but him. This was okay with me, because I didn't really like his friends and I was ashamed of my addiction again. I was happy to be reclusive and invisible, no more than an extension of him in the world of criminals and drug users.

There wasn't as much money in stolen cars as I expected. It was mostly loose change and sunglasses, and the occasional pack of gum from the cup holders. Nobody wanted to pay for a vehicle you had to start with a screwdriver. To support the many women in his life, my boyfriend went from one illegal scheme to another.

When things didn't go well, I was expected to pick up the slack. Which is why it didn't surprise me when he fell lengthwise across the bed as I was getting ready to work at the diner, telling me not to come home without two hundred dollars.

I was never going to make that selling omelets and coffee. With a sigh, I told him what I would do. I was going to go through the purses of the other waitresses and steal their wallets, and I'd meet him back at his mother's apartment. I'd known that I was going to do something like this eventually. Being a lowlife was just who I was, just like being an addict was a part of me, too.

"I better pick you up," he said, not wanting me to go anywhere else with the stolen money. When I walked out the door, he looked me up and down and said, "This is the perfect cover. You look just like a waitress!" I reminded him that I was a waitress, or at least I had been until today.

I quit my job by leaving out the back door without a word to anyone, running to a waiting car with stolen wallets in my hand.

I expected my heist to improve our relationship, but he took everything I had just stolen, dropped me off at his mother's, and left. "You must love him or you wouldn't stay," his mother told me that day. It was true. I loved him as much as I loved myself, and he also loved me as much as I loved myself.

At the end of the summer, we were pulled over by a fleet of police in a stolen car. He bolted out of the car door, attempting to make a run for it, but was tackled at the end of the street. I remained sitting in the passenger seat, waving goodbye and feeling strangely detached. I didn't even open the door to get out.

I was ejected from the vehicle by a gruff police officer, bent over the back of the cruiser and handcuffed.

I didn't want to go down without some sort of protest, so I started kicking.

"You can't arrest me!" I squeaked, "I'm starting school soon!"

"Oh yeah, what are you taking? Criminology 101?" He laughed, and carted me off to jail.

I was back, and I was going through the usual routine. Shower. Grey uniform. Booking. It was standard during intake to ask a long list of questions, one of which was "Are you or could you be pregnant?" To which I responded, "Yes, I'm pregnant. About to have a baby. In fact, I'm in early labor. Call a doctor."

Unimpressed, the corrections officer handed me a little cup to pee in. I tried to explain that I'd just been joking, that I certainly was not pregnant, and never would be, but she would have none of it. I was directed to the bathroom.

I returned the cup to her, and we both sat silently waiting for the results.

"Well, what do you know," she said, while I was staring at the wall. "Looks like you were right." She held up the positive pregnancy test for me to see, but I saw lines everywhere and to my untrained eyes this meant nothing.

"It's wrong," I told her. I explained why, and she agreed to do another test for confirmation. When that test also came back positive, I begged her for another test, to which she obliged.

There, sitting in a remand center, staring at three positive pregnancy tests on the desk of a corrections officer, I began to hope. I was alive. I must have looked as stupefied as I felt, because she threw her hands up, and, laughing, sent me to my unit.

I reacted to the news of my pregnancy with such an intensity of emotion that it altered my perception of reality. I walked through the halls of the jail as if I'd just stepped into a world where roses grew and birds sang. I was in a bubble, nothing could come against me, and the universe, aligning itself with the miracle that was my baby, seemed to unfold as I took each step.

I never thought about the timing, about preparation, about the ducks that weren't in a row. All I could see was the steady stream of brilliant light that had cut through the long darkness. The other inmates looked at me and knew. "It's a boy," one said, handing me an extra sandwich. "You'll be needing this."

A baby in jail is magic. Mothers with their own children they couldn't hold patted my stomach and saved extra meals for my baby and I. Hardened criminals sat beside me and told stories of their babies, and with a smile I would put my hand over my unborn baby and I knew that if they could love their children, I could do it too. Life was going to be great. Loving someone else was all you needed to survive, and I was going to survive.

The day before my court date, an older woman heating her dinner in the unit microwave offered me her meal and this advice: "You'll love your baby, but you have to love yourself, too. If you don't love yourself, you'll end up back here. You can do it. Just don't look back."

I was surprised. I couldn't remember anyone ever telling me to love myself. I wasn't sure if it was good advice, but I couldn't ignore it. It stayed with me. It was like she had unlocked my heart, and finding nothing where something should be, left me with this treasure and a bit of strength to cling to.

I plead guilty and begged the judge to allow me to serve my sentence in the community under house arrest. "She can stay with her mother," my lawyer offered, and the judge agreed. My conditions were drawn up. I hugged my lawyer and shook the hand of the guard who escorted me to my release, sure I would never be back.

I was right.

My mother came to get me, reminding me that she had a firm 'no drug' rule. "Don't worry," I told her, "I'm never going to do drugs again."

I never did.

I cheerfully wrote to my new co-parent, who was himself still in jail, to tell him of the great news. He responded with a few choice expletives, which I laughed off. "You'll come around," I told him. I was sure that once he'd had the chance to really let the good news sink in, he would be as delighted as I was. In the meantime, I would spend my days preparing for the arrival of the light and love of my life.

I attended the best prenatal classes I could afford. I lovingly cross-stitched monogrammed baby bedding. I rewarded my body for creating life by eating well and sleeping often. I devoured baby magazines and read and re-read *What To Expect When You're Expecting*. I went to probation. I deleted most of my friends list, refriended people, then deleted them again. I took ridiculously expensive prenatal vitamins. I had a labor plan, a life plan, and a savings account with almost one hundred dollars in it. My doctor felt that my pregnancy was going well and that I would soon give birth to a healthy baby.

I agreed with my doctor. I wasn't anxious over the fact that I was unemployed and single. I saw house arrest as a blessing, thinking of other women who had to work during their pregnancies. I would wake up every day overwhelmed with gratitude, in awe as my body grew and my baby took the best parts of me and created something new. I couldn't hate my body anymore, because my baby was inside it.

The past was the past, I told myself. Everything was going to change now. I refused to doubt, I had faith in my future and I intensely guarded my unborn baby like a gift.

My sort-of boyfriend was released from prison just before the birth of our child. He moved back into his mother's apartment, and called me at my mother's house.

"Have you ever thought of us being together?" he asked.

"I thought we were together," I replied.

"Sure, almost-wife," he said while taking a long drag from his cigarette and exhaling into the phone.

A few weeks later, I went into labor.

It was a clear and sunny afternoon in late spring when my daughter arrived in this world. She made her entrance to an audience of many, with my mother, my almost-mother-in-law, my almost-husband, my little sister, the doctor, the baby nurse, and a few residency students who had just stopped by, all clustered at the end of my open legs to watch as I became a mother.

I'd had an epidural, which followed nitrous oxide and a shot of morphine, so instead of screaming in pain, I thanked everyone for

coming and encouraged my almost-husband to get my good angle as he recorded the whole event on his iPhone.

My baby was beautiful and perfectly designed, with a shock of black hair just like mine had been. Everything about her was amazing. Her small hands curling around my fingers, her bright eyes drinking in the world around her, her cheeks smooth and round. She was just as delighted to be alive as I was to have her. My heart burst every time I looked at her.

My loyal girlfriends came to visit me at all hours of the night, each one claiming to be my sister to the hospital's front desk. Even my best gay friend came, and when he also claimed to be my sister, the receptionist came to my room with her eyebrows raised to ask just how many sisters I had.

"My parents are fundamentalist evangelicals," I explained. "They didn't believe in birth control." She rolled her eyes and let him through.

I proudly introduced my new baby girl to everyone, certain that she was the prettiest, the happiest, the best in every way. My friends all agreed, and I beamed and swaddled and changed diapers like I was the mother of a Queen.

I thought, when I was pregnant, that I had discovered love, that fate had handed me purpose and destiny disguised as a positive pregnancy test. But when I looked at my daughter for the first time, I knew that I had never loved until that moment. It was beautiful and terrifying. Terrifying because I had been hoping for a boy, and not just because everyone had told me it was a boy, and not because boys were better. Being the mother of a daughter was terrifying because I didn't know how to protect a little girl from all the horrible things that could happen to her.

I didn't know how to tell her that the world was scary for a girl, that she would always have to be afraid, just like me. I wondered if she would be smart and strong, which would make it especially hard for her. I wondered how many heartbreaks I would have to hold her through, how to teach her to hide and be less of herself to survive, but how to let her dream as much as society would allow her to dream.

"Bad things happen to boys all the time, too," said my almost-husband, assuring me that having a boy was just as dreadful as having a girl. I thought about his childhood and I couldn't disagree.

I brought my daughter home to my mother's house while my almost-husband went back to his mother's and recovered from the shock and stress of witnessing childbirth. For a week I did nothing but hold my baby and sleep, suffering happily from new love and exhaustion.

CHAPTER FIFTEEN

Craigslist

At the end of the week my almost-husband called and asked me to bring our daughter to his mother's so that his family could see her. I tried to convince him to come to *my* mother's house, but there was an intense, unspoken hatred between my mother and him and we agreed this was too awkward. I folded my little darling into her stroller and we made our way to her father.

I arrived to find his mother's boyfriend carting several unhinged doors into the apartment. He was an elderly man who was suffering from dementia, and as we later found out, a brain tumor. He had come upon these discarded doors while walking through the back alley. He excitedly asked around for the owner of these doors, and discovering that the building was undergoing renovations and that the doors were going to the city dump, he brought them one by one up three flights of stairs, where he arranged them in the hallway, labeled them "standing art" and slapped on a twenty dollar price tag.

When none of the other residents offered to purchase his art, he blamed it on their lack of sophistication and brought them all inside. He was certain he would find new homes for them on Craigslist. While whistling wartime radio tunes he busied himself creating online ads for the doors, pausing every once in a while to ask how the baby was doing. I sat on the couch and tried to encourage his artistic vision without breaking into laughter.

"Timeless! Classic!" I cheered, offering advertising suggestions. My almost-husband had already gotten bored with our daughter, who was taking a nap in her car seat, and he was on his laptop playing Farmville and helping the creative process by shouting more accurate descriptions for the doors such as "garbage" and "scrap wood."

When he didn't get any response online to the doors, the old man wondered aloud whether the rusted chain of a "vintage bathtub plug," found in the same ally, might do better.

"The only thing here of any value is my baby! You might as well put her on craigslist!" I replied.

Popping his head out from behind the Standing Art, the old man who was half gone and barely there laughed, understanding that this was a joke.

My almost-husband, seeing the opportunity to showcase his lack of boundaries by taking the joke one step further, abandoned his game and created a Craigslist posting himself.

For our daughter.

I felt as if I had just stepped on a landmine.

"You probably shouldn't," I said slowly, knowing that if I sounded too angry or too forceful it would only encourage him further. He was the enjoyable sort of man who liked to push buttons for his own amusement.

My pitiful objections made no difference. He pretended that he didn't hear me.

Type, type, type went the computer keys as I carefully packed up the diaper bag. Bang, bang, bang went the doors as they slid like dominos down the wall onto the floor, jolted by the errant hand of the old man. I watched my sleeping daughter open her eyes wide and cry, and my almost-husband, now finished with the computer, looked up and said, "I think she's hungry."

I picked her up to feed her, going over our departure in my mind. How to leave without a fight or a scene, that was the goal. The fallen doors were being repositioned so I took my baby into the next room and sat down to nurse her, knowing that being here, in this apartment with this family, was a mistake.

She had been fed, changed, and redressed when there was a loud knock on the door, followed by an ear-splitting crack as a S.W.A.T. team entered the apartment by kicking the door through. I held my baby in my arms as my almost-husband lunged towards the front door, cursing and screaming. He was handcuffed on the grounds of being a threat to himself, and while he was lying face down at gunpoint, I backed myself into a corner and hid behind a recliner with my daughter in my arms.

Seconds later, my daughter and I were surrounded. In a state of terror, I handed my daughter to the police officer who found us. She was lifted from my arms and then I myself was lifted up like a small child and taken out of the apartment.

When we reached the apartment lobby, my baby girl was gone, and I was standing empty-handed in front of a team of social workers and law enforcement.

I was in shock. I was separated from my baby for the first time, and I had no idea whether they planned to return my child to me or not. "Let me go with her, wherever you bring her, let me come!" I begged the social workers, but it soon became clear that she was being separated from me for her own protection, that my baby was not coming with me and I could not go with her.

I lost my mind. I sat on the sidewalk and sobbed, unable to answer questions or give a statement. It was heart-wrenching, soul-gutting grief, a pain that took away all sense and reason. I was put into a taxi by a police officer, who paid for my fare, and sent back to my mother's house. I only realized when I got there that the house keys were in the diaper bag. Numbly, I knocked, and my mother opened the door and saw me childless, tears streaming down my face. She could bring herself to say only one thing.

"Where is she?"

I'd spent years running from loneliness and pain. To me, the worst thing in the world was to feel negative emotions, and I'd avoided them by disconnecting and pouring drug after drug into the place where feelings belong.

Now, I was living and breathing pain. It was just as bad as I knew it would be. Yet, there was something else. There was, inside me, something stronger than fear, stronger than pain, stronger than rage and regret. It was love.

I understood that my daughter might be better in the arms of another mother. I believed that some other family might give her the life she deserved. But I knew that I could not live without her, and during every waking moment I renewed an internal vow to prove myself, to fight for my daughter until she was once again in my arms.

The next morning I answered a knock on the front door, and there stood my friend with a coffee in one hand and a newspaper in the other. He handed me the coffee first.

"Brace yourself," he cautioned, handing me the paper.

There, on the front page, was a picture of me in the hospital. Nothing can prepare you for being in the public eye. I had never been famous for anything, and now the worst moment of my life was front page news. To add to my horror, when I read the paper I discovered that not only had my almost-husband given an interview about our daughter, but he had said he was dating someone else, and that we had never been together.

What is going on with my life? I wondered. Then the phone rang.

It was the news reporter. "How could you take baby photos from Facebook?!" I demanded, "How could you use my daughter to sell papers?!" He said that if I didn't like anything that had been reported, now was my chance to set the record straight. "Could you make a statement regarding your child's father?" he asked.

"He's a bit of a dick," I explained, "but it was a joke. My daughter was never for sale."

"Excellent. Thank you for your time." he said.

The next day, the front-page headline read **CRAIGSLIST DAD A BIT OF A DICK**. I didn't know whether to laugh or cry.

I prepared myself for a long battle. I restrained from Googling myself. I stopped talking to my friends. I waited by the phone for the social worker to call, telling myself over and over again "You can get her back. You can get her back. You can get her back."

The social worker did call. She had called my doctor, my probation officer, and my mother, and she wanted to meet with me. I took a deep breath and braved through the reporters camped out on the front lawn, heading to what I was sure would be the toughest meeting of my life.

Luckily, good social workers don't gather evidence from newspapers. My social worker had read my criminal record, my history of drug use, and had heard of my house arrest. She had spoken to my probation officer, who said that I had followed my release conditions to the letter. She had spoken to my doctor, who had assured her that I had not been using drugs while pregnant. She had spoken to the team who had taken my daughter from me, who suggested that my problem might not be bad parenting as much as bad relationship choices.

I told her how my pregnancy had given me purpose. I explained how my baby had given me a reason to live and had helped my heart to heal. I begged her to let me see my child, and promised to do anything, absolutely anything, if she would let me live with my baby.

As she listened to me plead, I discovered that she was my friend. She wanted to give me and my daughter a life together. She believed that babies belonged with their mothers. She also wanted me to learn how to protect my child from danger, even if that danger was her other parent. I wanted to learn this, too.

When I knew that we were all on the same side, my social worker, my baby, and myself, I was able to give voice to other fears. Fears that had left me sleepless and full of doubt. Could recovering addicts raise children? Was this event going to ruin my daughter's life?

How could I become the kind of parent that my daughter deserved?

Was I going to make it? I needed to know.

Wanting to be better is half the battle, she told me. The other half is actually doing it. What happens between wanting to walk and taking the first step is up to you.

She closed my file and walked me to the door.

"What is the first step?" I asked before I left.

"Being here," she said.

The second step was going to Family Court.

The judge reviewed my file and made a decision. I would get my daughter back under a protection order. That meant that the courts would remain her legal guardians and I would be her caregiver. I was given a list of rules to follow, and if I could follow these rules for 90 days, I would be awarded guardianship and our file would be closed.

I was ecstatic. My lawyer and the social worker were less so. "This is the most extensive protection order I've ever seen," my lawyer told me, reading over the list of conditions. "I don't want to say that they're setting you up to fail, but…if you don't follow perfectly, you're going to lose your child again."

I had lived without my baby girl once, and I was never going to do it again. It didn't matter if the court had asked me to walk blindfolded across New York on a tightrope. I was going to do it, and I was going to do it well.

I was reunited with my daughter, and after I'd taken her home and breathed in her sweet baby smell and touched her soft baby face and promised her I'd never leave her again, I read over the list of conditions.

Protection Order:

Must not be outside after 10pm.

Must not let my child be in contact with criminals or those under the influence of drugs.

Must not let my child be in contact with her father.

These were just a few on a long list. While I tried to think of a strategy, ways to follow my 90-day Parenting Plan, one of my life-long friends offered me a room in her home. It was perfect. My friend loved me so much that she brought my daughter and I into her house, gave us our own room, made us family and gave me friendship. She had her own newborn, and we listened to each other's babies cry and we saw each other doing our best and we both agreed that this was hard, but that *we could do it.*

She never offered to make my life easier. She never suggested that I leave my daughter in better hands while I got a grip. She saw that my fragile hope and my precious baby were all that I had, and she pulled me alongside of her in her own journey through motherhood and made me feel like a sister. Being together, with my baby and my friend, and her baby and her lovely husband who made us dinner every night after he had worked all day, it was the best kind of love. It was the kind of love that made me stronger.

CHAPTER SIXTEEN

All Hail The Queen

When my trial run at parenting was finished, I returned to court and was awarded full custody of my daughter. To celebrate, I took her on her first road trip along the coast, to my family reunion. There, I showed off my baby to my American relatives, who tried not to read Canadian news stories if they could help it and were just grateful that none of their friends in the U.S. had heard of the Craigslist fiasco. They didn't know I was going to write a book.

It was on this vacation, sitting at a sunny internet café with my sleeping daughter in the stroller beside me, that I got a message from an old friend. She had been one of my drug sisters, someone who had tried to show me how to be bad without getting into trouble. I was a slow learner, but she had loved me anyway. When she left to get sober and start her own new life, she kept a close eye on all the people she had left behind. I was one of them. She wasn't my drug sister anymore, she was my sister friend.

She was writing me to tell me some bad news. My ex-almost-husband's mother's boyfriend, old Mr. Standing Art, had just passed away from a brain aneurysm. She knew I had gone three months without talking to my ex-almost-husband, but she thought I should know. The wake would be in one week, she said, just in case I wanted to go. She gave me the time and the address, just in case I felt like bringing my daughter to pay respects to the other side of the family. Just in case.

I had personally vowed never to speak to him again. I'd also promised this to my baby girl, who had smiled and crinkled her chubby cheeks in agreement. Taking her to the funeral was out of the question. What if I saw him? Of course I would. What if I had to speak to him? Of course, that would only be appropriate. What if I made a scene? No. If I did go, I would be above making the funeral a personal vendetta, a chance to finally speak my mind.

I marked the date and bought an outfit.

I hope they have tiny sandwiches, I messaged my sister friend.

They will, she wrote back.

She'd known I was going to go and had offered to cater the wake in lieu of attending, and she also knew how much I liked sandwiches.

I swept into the room with my daughter in my arms. With lowered eyelids I expressed condolences, scanning the room for my ex-almost-husband. He was nowhere to be seen. To fend off anxiety and grief, I took a handful of sandwiches off a tray and shoved them into my mouth. Still chewing, I turned and found the man I was looking for.

He was contrite, apologetic, soft-spoken and repentant. The death of someone who had practically been his stepfather had shaken the man. He was desperate for another human being to love him. He wanted nothing more than to be a part of his daughter's life. If only I would give him another chance, he said through tears, he would do whatever it took to make amends for his mistakes. He would never touch another drug. He would live the rest of his days proving to me and my daughter how much he loved us.

I watched him say all the things I never believed I'd hear, and I believed him. I wanted him to be the person he said he would be, for himself, for his daughter, for me. I believed in second chances and I especially believed in tears. I had never seen a man cry, and now here he was, crying and saying sorry. I was so moved that I slept with him.

I left thinking that the sex had probably been a mistake. A few short weeks later, I sat in the doctor's office, looking at a positive pregnancy test, then to my four month old daughter, then to the doctor. Nobody said a word. I was handed a little slip of paper with a list of local abortion clinics and sent back out into the unbelievable and uncertain territory of my own life.

I walked around city blocks, pushing the stroller and thinking about my future. I was once again single. All the sad and beautiful things my once-again-ex had said at the funeral had been forgotten by all except me. I had tried to remind him, to help him back to the place where he wanted better things, but it only made him angry. How could I be so stupid, we both wanted to know.

Was it right to intentionally bring a child into this world, knowing that it would be a struggle? Was one child not enough? Would two babies be more than I could handle? What if this pregnancy was a terrible, terrible mistake? What if a million things.

I stopped talking to myself and called a friend who was also a single mother. I knew she would give me unbiased advice, and I knew she'd hold my hand or watch my daughter if I chose to have an abortion.

She listened to me explain the situation and urged me to consider the daughter I already had. "Think about your child," she began.

"Yes, of course," I said.

"Don't you want to give your daughter the best life?" she asked.

"Of course." I replied. I knew I had called the right person.

"Then don't have an abortion," she said.

"Wait – what??"

Had I mistakenly called one of my old church friends?

"This might be your only chance to give your daughter a biological sibling. Your daughter was God's gift to you. Now you can give her a gift, someone who can grow up to be her best friend in this crazy world." she explained.

I said goodbye and sat in silence. It wasn't me and baby girl anymore. It was me and baby and baby. It was a lot. I was nervous. I was scared. I knew in the deepest part of me that my friend was right, and that I was going to be a mother of a *family.*

I decided to keep my new baby a secret until it was too late to change my mind. The more people who knew, the more people who could talk me out of it. I didn't want any negativity bringing me down. At night I rocked my daughter and instead of singing songs or saying nursery rhymes, I chanted "we can do this, we can do this" softly and slowly.

I think we both knew that it was true.

When I finally told my friends and family, I did it like a regular birth announcement, not a sad-single-mom-in-a-scary-place announcement.

"I'm excited and delighted," I told my friends, who stared and stuttered and eventually walked away speechless. I was only mildly annoyed by their lack of enthusiasm.

The only person who seemed to take this news in stride, almost as if he was not surprised, was my father. He was in Winnipeg, his newest military posting, and all he said was, "Would you and my granddaughter like to come visit me for Christmas?"

He paid our fare and met us at the airport, loving me and my daughter like we were the light of his life. I was so happy, all I could think to say was, "Hey, do you have more grey hairs?"

Christmas is absolutely my favorite time of year. It's a holiday all about love, and best of all, it's spoken in my love language: gifts. What could be better than being trapped inside, cozy and warm with the people you love, surrounded by presents? There's something magical that happens when your heart is full and you are surrounded by your favorite food and friends. It's just like being on drugs. You get high on love and friendship.

Christmas is so great, that if you wanted to convince me to do something crazy, that would be the time. I probably wouldn't say no. Even if that crazy thing was "Bethany, move to Winnipeg and start your entire life over." This is what my father said to me when I was sitting by the warm fire in his nice house, with his new wife, my little sister and my daughter by my side. "Winnipeg is perfect!" I told him. It was fifty below zero.

It wasn't until I returned to Vancouver to pack that I realized this was going to be a big deal. I was leaving all the people who had gotten me this far, and I was going to be living in my own apartment for the first time in my entire life. I was a mother of one, almost two children, and here I was standing on the edge of adulthood.

I almost didn't go. Being an adult is scary when you're looking in from the outside.

Who wants to live in Winnipeg? I asked myself.

Nobody, my rational mind told me.

But then another part of me, the new part, the one that came alive the same day my daughter was born, began to speak.

Don't you want to see if you can *do this by yourself? Don't you want to claim space in this world – to be alive long enough to make a home? Don't you want to try – just once – and see if you can stand by yourself, carrying your children on your own and facing the world like a warrior?*

It's hard to argue with that voice. When the call to battle comes from within, you can't ignore it. When your body tells you to live, to go, to stand, to be brave and strong and free, you just cannot stay where you are.

So I sold everything I owned, bought a ticket to Winnipeg, Manitoba, and boarded a plane with my baby girl, clinging to the diaper bag like it was the very last thing I had to hold. Which, of course, it was.

The day after I landed, I borrowed my father's car while he was at work and started to look for apartments. I found a two-bedroom condo that would fit all three of us, me and my babies, so I signed a lease and handed over the last of my money.

What am I going to do about groceries? I thought as I sat outside my new apartment. *And furniture? And everything else we would need to live?*

I talked to my father about it later that night, and he suggested social assistance.

"Welfare!" I said, incredulously.

"That's what it's there for. To help out people just like you." He said, "It would make paying taxes easier if I knew part of that money was going to help you."

It was never my dream, but the next day I went to the welfare office. When you have nothing and no way to get more, welfare doesn't seem like a bad idea. In fact, I was grateful. It turns out I wasn't the only single mother who needed help, and they had designed an assistance program just for single mothers with no education and no parenting skills. I couldn't believe my luck.

Not only did I get money every month to pay my rent, but I was given enough for groceries as well. I was able to save, and once a month I bought a furniture item from the thrift store. By the time my due date came, I had a bed and a kitchen table, as well as plates, knives and forks. I was tremendously proud of my beginning.

I discovered that painting was the cheapest and easiest way to decorate. I was nine months pregnant when I painted our entire apartment pink, blue and green. I didn't love it, but I figured that in another month I could buy some more paint and make it better. I didn't have a computer or internet, so I didn't know about Pinterest or DIY blogs. In the grocery store, I stood in the checkout line with my diapers and milk and read Oprah magazines, trying to figure out how to make my apartment a palace.

One day, the palace got a new Queen. I put my firstborn daughter to bed and labored by myself until the early morning hours, bracing against the hallway arc during contractions and wishing with everything in me that I had already gotten an epidural. When I couldn't take it any longer, I called my stepmother. My father was on tour in Afghanistan, so she brought over my little sister to stay with my sleeping daughters, and then took me to the hospital.

I got my epidural. I took a nap. And then, at the break of dawn, my second daughter entered the world. She was breathtaking. Just like her older sister, she was the most beautiful baby I had ever seen. She had big blue eyes, rosebud lips, and a doughy little face. And, just like her older sister, and just like me, she had dark hair that stood straight up. I never knew I could love someone as much as I loved my first baby, but in one moment, my heart grew, and my family grew, and I loved everyone so much I could hardly bear it.

Then she opened her little pink lips and screamed. She was ferocious. She knew what she wanted and when she wanted it, and she was equipped with the strength and endurance to get what she wanted handed to her. Bless her heart. It had taken me years to figure out how to be heard, and she'd been born with this amazing ability. I was in awe.

CHAPTER SEVENTEEN

Bail Conditions

I called my girls' father from the delivery room to congratulate him on the birth of his second child. He was taken aback – he thought for sure he was going to have a son.

"Since you named our first daughter without me, can I at least name this one?" he asked.

A slight wave of guilt rushed up to speak before I could say no. I had been feeling bad about how I'd taken our first child away and then moved her across the country without asking him. Now, I'd had our second child in a city he couldn't visit. He'd never even been on a plane. I knew he would never come. Since I'd abandoned him, the least I could do was give him some connection to her.

"Sure," I told him. "Let me know when you decide."

"Hold on," he said, then, speaking to someone else, he said, "Babe, what was your name again?"

I gritted my teeth.

"Tina Colada," he said, laughing. "I had to wake her up to ask her."

I tried to choke out a response but I was interrupted.

"Calm down." he rumbled, "I'll let you know our daughter's name when I get there."

"Wait – when are you coming?!" I asked, but he had already hung up.

Don't let him get to you, I thought, trying to talk myself down from a panic attack. *He's trying to mess with your head to get a reaction.*

I turned my attention back to my new baby girl. I discharged myself, brought my beautiful daughter back to our condo and introduced her to her older sister. It's hard to say who loved her more, me or my firstborn. We were in a reverie. Her first night at home, we made a big nest out of blankets and pillows and snuggled there, together, my little family and I.

Four days later, my girls' father arrived. He was too nervous to come alone, with the cops at the airport and him being high, so he brought his mother and his four best friends with him. He dropped his mom off at my apartment and went to find a hotel for himself and his extra baggage.

His mother was not impressed. She looked around and saw not how much I'd saved to buy what little I had, but only what little I had. How could I live in such poverty? I didn't even have a couch. Where was she going to sleep, in the big blanket nest with me and the girls? She was beside herself.

She called her son.

"Bethany has nothing! I've seen trailers with more furniture than this! Even homeless people have nicer belongings!" She was hysterical.

"You didn't even notice the interior decorating I've done," I said, pointing out my paint job and mentioning how, when you didn't steal or do crime for money, things tended not to just show up in your house. You had to buy them, and sometimes that took time.

"I've heard enough," she said, and went outside to chain smoke until a solution to my desperate situation was found.

I tried to ignore her as I focused on my girls. I worried about feeding them and bathing them and putting them into clean clothes. I tried to ignore the five big screen televisions that showed up a few hours later, along with a big freezer, a set of dinnerware, towels, power tools, and steaks.

I cleaned the girls' room and rocked them to sleep while others set up my house the way they thought it should be. Nobody knew how proud I was of how far I'd come since arriving with nothing. Nobody would have cared if they did know, because in that world, you are proud of what you own. The more the better. Paying for something when you didn't have to wasn't something to brag about. It was stupidity.

A month later, my house was full. Full of people I didn't like, full of things I didn't want, full in a thousand ways that were wearing me down. I needed to get out of there. I put my babies in their new double stroller and took them to the park, and when I came home I couldn't even open the front door. Someone had just come back with too many boxes of big electronics.

I called the girls' father and begged him to get the stuff out of my house and to give me some space.

"I can't live here, our children can't live here. This isn't a home anymore, it's a storage locker." I complained.

"Storage locker, good idea," he said. "We'll trade for a night. You can stay at the hotel with the girls, and I'll get everything out of the house and move it into storage."

With a sigh, I made a path through the boxes in my kitchen, grabbed the diaper bag and a change of clothes, and took a cab to his hotel. I put the girls to sleep and spent the night staring out the window, trying to think of a way to get things back to the way they should be. It was a lot easier to leave than to make someone else leave, but I'd just had a baby and I didn't want to run from a place I'd just moved into. I wasn't sure what to do.

The next morning, I called to see how the moving was going. No answer. I waited until lunch time, no answer. I asked the front desk how long the hotel room had been rented for. Check-out was in one hour. I looked around at his things scattered everywhere, and decided to leave them for him to sort out. I ordered room service, had lunch, and then took the bus back home with my baby girls.

My apartment had two police cars parked outside, and my front door had been sealed off. "This is a crime scene, you can't go in there," I was told.

I looked at the yellow tape. I should have walked away, but instead I said "Can I just go inside and get some new diapers for my little girl?"

"Do you live here?" I was asked.

"Well, I did," I said.

"You're going to have to come with us, Ma'am."

My stepmother came to get my baby girls, and I was taken down to the police station and charged with Possession of Property Obtained By Crime.

I was released on bail, and when I returned to my apartment, it was just as empty as it had been before everyone arrived. No televisions, no power tools, no people. It was a mess, but it felt like mine. I looked around and smiled, knowing that everything was once again right, and that everyone who shouldn't have been there was gone.

I cleaned and bleached and washed and folded, and when everything was in its place, I went to get my girls from my anxious stepmother. That night we snuggled together and my oldest baby slept through the night for the first time.

I had never been released on bail. In my old life, I would have gone straight to jail. In my old life, I would have done the crime. I didn't think I had done anything illegal. I didn't know what my charge meant, other than it indicated I'd had stolen property in a home where I lived. Since I didn't buy the items, and didn't ask for them, I didn't think it was illegal. I tried explaining this to my pro-bono lawyer, who just looked at me sadly.

"The only way you could have escaped this charge is if you had turned him in before the cops got him," he said, noting that failing to prevent or discourage crime was also illegal.

"It would have been easier to kill him than turn him in," I said, half-joking.

"There's not a jury in this country that would convict you," he replied, half-joking, then, "Maybe he'll take the blame and you won't end up going to court."

I wondered how many career criminals this guy knew. Probably none. Nobody I knew would take the blame if there was a chance they could stay out of jail. I was going to court. What I wasn't going to do was show up and hope for the best. I was going to *be* the best. Court was in one year, and in that year, I was going to do everything I could to make myself the opposite of a criminal girlfriend.

I called up my sister-friend, the one who sent me to the funeral and was, as I told her, responsible for me even having a second daughter. "I can't go to jail," I told her, and she agreed. We brainstormed. We made lists. Together, we thought of a plan. I was going to take my babies and bring them to the one place known for redemption. The Church.

"The worst that will happen is you'll be bored or be judged. The best thing that will happen is you will find new friends and become a better person. If you want to stay *out* of trouble, you have to stay *away* from trouble."

"I don't have anything to wear to church," I told her.

Before Sunday came around, she had mailed me a new pair of boots and a jacket.

"It doesn't matter what you wear underneath," she said. "Just tell people you get cold easily."

I called up my stepmother, who had been praying hard ever since she'd come to my rescue and watched my babies while I was at the police station. When I asked if I could go to church with her on Sunday, she just about burst into tears.

We went every week, and by April I'd had my girls baptized in the Anglican church. It was beautiful and it made me feel like I had contributed to their spiritual lives. No matter what, they would be together in heaven, and if they lived long lives and died old and happy, they would be together in this world, too. I sighed happy sighs and tried to get comfortable on the pew.

My father returned from his tour of duty, and after meeting his new granddaughter and sleeping in his own bed, he sat me down to give me some terrible news. He wanted me to go to a *new church*. He had noticed that my children were the only children at the Anglican parish. He had noticed that everyone there was thirty years older or thirty years younger than I was, and that my only friends were *my own children*.

I had also noticed this. It was what I loved about it. The last thing I wanted was to go to a church where I might be forced to meet people my own age. It sounded horrible. Old ladies who crocheted blankets for orphans and sang out of hymnals were adorable. Women's Bible Studies and Beth Moore DVD's were just the worst. I didn't want to go anywhere that would encourage friendship or commitment and I certainly didn't want to go anywhere with people who were too excited or too happy. Organists and stained glass windows, yes. Worship teams and church retreats, no.

My father believed he knew best, and the next Sunday he picked me up in his truck and brought me to a junior high school gymnasium. My stepmother had been driving home from yoga and had seen a sign on the street corner advertising a Sunday morning service. The church was called Oasis. She and my father agreed it was perfect.

I signed my girls into the Sunday School program, which was full of bright eyed little girls and boys. I walked past rows of school lockers and found a table with candy and Starbucks coffee, which they were giving away *for free.* Armed with sugar and caffeine, I entered a dark gymnasium where a band was playing with neon spotlights and a smoke machine. I couldn't sing along because I'd never heard the song before, so I sipped my coffee and tried to look around for evidence of speaking in tongues or the tell-tale signs of evangelical enthusiasts, raised hands, closed eyes, and a barely perceptible swaying to the music. There was none of these things.

The sermon was like a TED talk. Short and sweet and easy to listen to, and the pastor occasionally read notes off his iPhone. When it was over, nobody rushed to greet me or asked if I was new. Everyone was new. It was the church for non-churched people. I returned to the Sunday School room to pick up my baby girls, who presented me with artwork, their happy little faces beaming with pride.

"Do you want to go back?" my stepmother asked over lunch.

"Well, it seemed like it was good for the kids," I said, "And I never say no to free coffee."

She smiled, my babies smiled, and we all came back the next week. By the time my court date came around, church wasn't just a part of my stay-out-of-jail plan. It was a part of my life.

CHAPTER EIGHTEEN

Not A Cage

The day had finally come. I stood beside my lawyer as he cited my regular church attendance and tried his best to convince the judge I was normal.

"Normal people don't support their families by doing crime," the Judge told me as I balanced my baby in one arm and my toddler in the other. I knew he was right, and it made me want to cry. "And next time, don't bring your kids with you to court." he added.

"There won't be a next time," I said. Nobody believed me anymore. I plead guilty to the Possession of Stolen Property charge and was sentenced to nine months of house arrest and eighty hours of community service.

But written into the conditions of my house arrest was this exception: on Sunday mornings, I was allowed to leave the house for no longer than three hours to attend church.

I tried not to see my house as a cage. I tried to remember that my peers, the ones who'd made better life choices, were back at work after having their babies and I was at home, existing off the money they paid in taxes. I tried to remember that many stay-at-home moms, the ones who weren't on house arrest, also spent most of their time inside with their babies and toddlers, and that I was lucky to be among the mothers who could say that they not only saw their children's childhood unfold, but created the magic that made it happen.

I pushed my need for freedom and contact with the outside world deep down inside me and gave my girls all I could. We painted and colored and napped. We sat criss-cross on the floor and ate snacks and sang made-up baby songs. I crafted a schedule that included all the recommended facets of a good childhood: art, reading, sleep, healthy foods, and at least twenty minutes outside every day. Not for myself, of course. I opened my back door and my girls had picnics in the sun, crawling around on the green grass while I stood in the door frame and watched the traffic go by our house, willing myself not to wish I had somewhere I could go.

Church became the Grand Event. I started preparing for Sunday on Saturday morning. I'd iron our outfits and wash our hair, fluttering around with the excitement of being able to leave the house. On Sunday morning we were ready and waiting by the front door a half-hour before my dad came to pick us up. We were going to church.

I'd learned that the best way to be at church was to be invisible. This way, nobody would ask us for play dates we couldn't go on, and nobody would wonder where my husband was, or where I worked. I didn't want to answer any of these questions. Besides that, if we left as soon as church was over, I'd have time to go to the grocery store and buy food for the week. Sunday became the day of gathering, of equipping myself with the tools needed to sustain my family for the week ahead. In church, it was my soul that was filled, and on the way home, it was my fridge.

Even though I didn't talk at church, I listened. I heard everything. At first, I took bits and pieces from the message like the wary child I was, waiting to see if the words would make me sick before I took another bite. One day I said to my father, "I don't think this pastor has lied even once."

"That's a strange way to put it," my stepmother noted, but to me it wasn't strange. I'd been expecting something toxic but had gotten something whole. I heard things like the power of forgiveness. How to love others well. The beauty of serving others. The importance of relationships. When not to give up. When to give in.

I took these gems and adorned myself with them, using beautiful truths to disarm the sadness that plagued me during the week. Monday was always a great day. The words from Sunday were still fresh in my mind. I felt strong and capable. What was house arrest? Nothing. When it was over, I was going to make up for lost time and my girls and I were going to live amazing lives.

Tuesday was an okay day. Deep breaths and firm resolve took over the cheery ways of Monday. I was a little battle weary, although I usually had something from Sunday to cling to, if not for the strength to overcome, then for the strength to endure. *Everyone makes mistakes,* I would tell myself. *You're a good mother. You'll make it.* More deep breaths.

Wednesday was a struggle. Were my children missing out on life by being trapped inside with me? Were they at a disadvantage by having me as their mother? I thought of all the places I had been by the age of three, and how my children rarely made it out of the front door. What was going to happen to them? Were we going to be okay? I didn't know anymore.

By Thursday or Friday, I was a wreck. I knew that who I was, was not enough. I feared that my children would grow up to be just like me. I wanted them to be so much more, but I could see that they loved me, that they walked and talked and lived like me, and it frightened me. I imagined their futures and saw two other versions of me in this world. How could I stop this from happening?

I couldn't live without my children, but I was not going to be enough for them. I didn't want them to define themselves using me as a yardstick, to see themselves in the light of my own negative self-image. My fear of having daughters stemmed from my fear of being a woman, but here we were, three little women living under the shadow of my house arrest. I knew that if I wanted my girls to be more, I would need to be more, and I didn't have a clue how to make that happen. There was only one place I could go.

I didn't want to be the type of person that loved church. I was far more comfortable fighting it. I was going to church because the girls loved it, because it was the one place we could go, because I needed to see people and watch adults talk just to remember what it was like. But slowly, I realized that I needed more than church. I needed to be more of myself, and to do that, I needed God to show me who I was.

I began to see that these beautiful buildings with stained-glass windows and altars, and the dark gymnasiums with neon lights and smoke machines, were nothing more than four corners and four walls. The real magic happened inside of you, not in a church. My guard had been up because I knew I could be hurt, but you could get hurt anywhere.

I wondered what might happen if I let my guard down. Could I be helped? Could I trust God?

These questions made me nervous, and I looked around for a distraction. This distraction was six feet two inches tall and living in an eight foot cell. It was my girls' father, who wrote me from jail every day and called me just as often. He was as lonely and lost inside his own head as I was. He was just as sad. He was cut off from the outside world by a jail cell, and I was cut off from the outside world by my own front door, and neither one of us could make new friends to fill that void.

Strange things happened in my mind when I only had one person to tell my thoughts to. The desire for connection became more important than trustworthiness or the way I had been treated. I needed to be heard, even if it was by someone I thought I hated. I wanted us to be together imperfectly instead of being perfect apart. I became less and less afraid of him. He couldn't hurt my children because he was in jail. What he could do was listen, and he did.

Once I had been heard by him, another strange thing happened. I couldn't hate him. Even if I should have, even though there were so many reasons to, I didn't. We can't hate the people we know. So when he wanted to be heard by me, I listened. What could we do now that we knew each other's secrets? We had to be friends.

I saw both our broken hearts, I saw our little girls, I saw the difficult future, and I knew that one of us had to get help if any of us were to have a chance. I also knew it would have to be me, and I had a feeling I knew where help was going to come from.

I got on my knees late one night and prayed for the first time in a long time. I had a deal to make with God. I knew that I myself had nothing to offer. I knew that I'd worn out my welcome at Heaven's gates. I didn't think God would listen to someone like me, praying for things I didn't deserve, so I brought the best I had to offer. My children.

 I would, I bargained with God, raise my little girls as Christian. I would never say another bad thing about the church. I would take them to church every Sunday *even after I was released from house arrest,* and I would do everything right from now on if only God would help me raise my babies.

I needed to know how to keep them from harm. In return, I would teach them not to harm others. I wanted my children to be blessed, and if God could make that happen, I would teach them how to be a blessing. I wanted my children to grow up strong and brave and full of love for the world, and if God could draw the best out of their father and I so that we could teach these little girls how to live this way, I would dedicate my life to being the best Christian non-Christian there was.

I prayed until my mind was empty. With all my worries hanging in the air instead of in my heart, I wondered how to expect a response. Should I have asked for a sign? Rustling leaves blowing a nice cool breeze into my bedroom: we had a deal. Earthquake: no deal.

No wind or waves or quakes happened, and I lay in bed and began to drift off to sleep. But then, a song came to me, in the slow, soft voice of my own mother. It was a song she had sung to me when I was a baby.

The Lord bless you and keep you. The Lord make his face to shine upon you and be gracious, and give you peace. Amen.

"Hope begins in the dark,

the stubborn hope that if you just

show up and try to do the right thing,

the dawn will come.

You wait and watch and work:

you don't give up."

Anne Lamott, *Bird by Bird: Some Instructions on Writing and Life*

CHAPTER NINETEEN

The Great Love Experiment

There is power in a mother's prayer, and it doesn't matter who that mother is. I woke up the next morning, not with the weight of my mistakes, but with a sense of peace and *togetherness.* I felt like God and I were a team, like all of a sudden I could do all of the difficult things before me, and not only was I going to do them, but I was going to enjoy the challenge. I was excited about my small, house-bound life.

Without meaning to, I started talking to God in my head. I liked the feeling of emptying my emotions instead of burying them. It didn't feel like praying, so I told myself it wasn't. A non-religious person such as myself didn't pray on a regular basis, anyway. Rather, I felt like I was having a conversation with a very wise friend. And that friend just happened to be God.

The first thing I wanted to know was what I should do about my past. Should I feel guilty about everything – everything I had ever done that made me a bad parent and a bad person? I asked God.

Guilt is terrible, God told me. *Feeling bad for the hurt you've caused others is empathy, and empathy looks for solutions. Guilt looks for blame and fosters self-hate. Can you change the past by hating yourself?* I wanted to say yes, but the answer seemed like no.

Why don't you try to look for a story about love and forgiveness, God suggested, *and think about these things instead?*

Where would I find a story about that?

That Sunday, the pastor stood on the stage with aqua blue lights and the smoke machine and his iPhone Bible app and spoke about love and forgiveness. He told a story about a man who loved his family so much that he was constantly forgiving them for being jerks. They were the worst group of people, liars, cheaters, drunks, and losers. Some of them seemed okay, there were a few lawyers and politicians, but in reality, those guys were the meanest. They hurt him, and he forgave them, and the strange part was that he didn't feel any shame for being walked all over, or regret forgiving them one too many times. What did he do instead?

He held his sister's hair back when she was hung-over and throwing up into the toilet. He gave his mom money for groceries after she'd spent all her money at Bingo. When his brother ran out of gas, he walked to the gas station with a can and brought back enough gas so his brother could get home. When his brother went to the bar instead, he stayed up to make sure he came back safely. He found out who his father owed money to, and he went and repaid the debt. He knew his family was a mess, but he loved them.

I got this story. I wanted to meet this guy. I felt like we would get along. I seemed like the exact type of person he would like to help.

"This story is straight out of the Bible," the pastor said. *Ridiculous,* I thought to myself. *How could I not see that coming.* I hated obvious and predictable stories, even more so when I couldn't predict them. There was nothing to do now but get a Bible and read it.

On the way back home, I asked my dad if he had a Bible.

"This is just so that I can look something up. It's for information. It's nothing more than a tool." I assured him that I didn't really want the Bible, I only wanted to read it. I would be happy to give it back once I was done.

"I do have one," my father told me. "It's a military edition, and I think it's the same version your pastor uses."

"What one is that?" I asked.

"The Message." my dad said. I was delighted. When The Message Bible was first printed, my mother refused to read it, saying it was for idiots and blasphemers. I was going to read it cover to cover.

Even with all my years of religious upbringing, I had never read the Bible myself. There didn't seem a need when I was surrounded by others who could quote it word for word. I knew the basics – creation, sin, death, sin, shame, sin, more death, the resurrection, ending with eternal servitude or eternal damnation. I thought this was the light version. I told myself I would not take it sugar-coated any longer.

To make sure I wouldn't miss anything, I started at the beginning. I read it like a story, a metaphor for creation and beginnings. I saw the struggle of humanity and the loss of hope, the gift of forgiveness and the power of love, the passion and the frailty of humanity all wrapped up in a beautiful book that told story after story of lives that were so different than my own, but of a condition so much the same; that of needing to be loved and needing to love. A few lapses in judgment aside, such as the flood and that messy business with Egypt, it seemed like God knew what he was doing.

The best part of the Bible was Jesus. The Jesus story sounded suspiciously like the nice guy with the crazy family. I could feel a life lesson coming on, and I was ready for it. *Use your imagination,* I told myself, *pretend this was real. What would this story tell you about love?*

I thought about all the people I loved. The list was so short, and the worst thing about this tiny list was that I couldn't love the people on it as much as they deserved. I thought about all the people I didn't love. That was a much longer list. In fact, it never ended. I challenged myself to find a balance, to discover a way to make one list longer and the other shorter.

I didn't have to look far or wait long. My girls' father phoned, and as I talked to him about my day and told him all the amazing things our daughters had done, I wondered what list he was on. He was somewhere in the middle, between exasperation and understanding, the small line between friend and enemy. *What would I even say to him to get him over to the love side?* I wondered. I felt as if I owed it to my girls to love their father.

I would tell him how I understood why his heart was broken, that my own heart had been broken too. I would tell him how I believed that everyone could be made unbroken, that I had seen enough good in him to know that he could make it if he tried. I would forgive him, I would say, and the things he had done would be forgotten, and I would let him come into my world and be a part of my family. I would love him, and together we would be better. I would tell him many things I didn't know were true until I said them. I thought about it, and figured I had better also let him know that my strict dating standards had risen and now included such qualifications as having a legitimate job, remaining sober, and abstaining from all criminal activity.

I couldn't say any of this. I was always a better writer than a conversationalist, so I wrote it in a letter. I really wasn't sure how he would take it. I mailed the letter and waited in that awful space of time where you are vulnerable and uncertain and waiting for another person to respond. Eventually, he did.

Love sounds great, he wrote back.

It really does, doesn't it? I replied.

We started our last attempt at a relationship.

The Great Love Experiment had began.

He was released early for good behavior, arriving on my doorstep a few days before my own house arrest ended. I welcomed him with a copy of his new resume, one I had created using words like "construction expert" and "certified welder" instead of "career criminal" and "just released from prison".

"I'm not qualified for any of these jobs," he pointed out.

"Yes, but ninety percent of success is your attitude. I've seen you start a stolen car with a paper clip. You can hammer a few nails together and make a building." I felt I was being very supportive.

My father took him out to buy a toolbox and steel-toed boots. I waited at home while my boyfriend and my father went ahead with my plan, my father standing beside a man he never thought he'd see again and my boyfriend standing beside a man who he thought he could never be. I hoped it would be magical.

I spent my first free days after house arrest at my father's so I could look on his computer for jobs. I was optimistic. So many people wanted to hire construction experts. It was a good thing my boyfriend was a fast learner, because none of his references would check out. I hoped he'd just impress them with his work ethic.

He got a job. The girls and I watched from the patio as he took his toolbox and went off into the world of the gainfully employed. I was confused when this didn't make him happy. I couldn't understand why he hesitated before leaving every morning, wavering at the door like he was going to battle instead of a construction site. I loved him in the same way I had been loved, by encouraging him to try harder and to be better.

When he got his first paycheck, he bought a laptop and started looking for new work. He had tried things my way and didn't need any more fake resumes, he said. He was getting frustrated with my type of love. It was on a particularly hard day, a day where everyone had failed him and nobody was on his side, that he found something that was destined to make his bad day worse.

He was rifling through the cupboard for cigarettes when he found my birth control prescription. He couldn't believe it. What kind of sneaky, slutty whore uses birth control? The kind that cheats on her boyfriend when he's in jail? The kind that lies and says she loves you but doesn't want to get pregnant? He knew I was always that kind of stupid slut. He found the cigarettes and lit one in the kitchen.

I tried to tell him that I'd never cheated. If he'd calm down, he'd remember that I had just been on house arrest, and that we already had two kids and I wasn't trying to do anything but plan ahead and make reasonable decisions. Besides, I told him, if we were going to have another baby, didn't he think we should be married first?

"It's that fucking cult church you go to," he yelled, grinding the cigarette between his teeth. "Well NOBODY is going to tell ME when I can have kids! And NO RELIGION is going to tell ME when I should get married! There's only ONE FUCKING PERSON WHO MATTERS. I AM GOD IN THIS FAMILY."

"Can you at least smoke outside?" I asked, reminding him that our youngest daughter had asthma. He stormed outside to finish his cigarette and I locked the door behind him.

That will teach him to talk to me like that! I thought, giving my best stink-eye to the turned lock.

He kicked the door down and sucker-punched me in the ribs. When I didn't respond he said, "You sure don't have a lot to say now, do you." He threw the birth control in the garbage and walked away to find something to hold the front door together.

Relationships are hard.

When I finally caught my breath, I mumbled in his direction "I'm pretty sure you broke my rib."

"Well. Maybe I did, and maybe I didn't." He replied, taking a long drag on his fresh cigarette. "I'll take you down to the hospital and get you x-rays if you want. But if it turns out not to be broken after we go all the way down there, I'm going to bring you back here and break it."

"I think you should move out," I told him.

He didn't, but he did move to the couch that night. The next day, he didn't go to work. He didn't leave the house and his eyes didn't leave me. He was waiting for me to leave, and he was waiting to fight me over it.

He got a call saying he'd been fired for not showing up right after a call from his mother saying she couldn't pay him back the money she had just borrowed. He broke the phone against the wall and summoned me. He had no more money and he needed my bank card for cigarettes, he said.

"What about groceries? What about diapers?" I asked, pointing out that since he had no more money, my money from welfare was all we had.

"If you're hungry, go steal something to eat." he told me.

I refused, and he put his head into his hands and said, "I liked you better when you just did what you were told."

This isn't love. I thought, and I was right. I was kicked and punched until I couldn't stand straight or see anything.

"Mommy is in a time-out," he told my crying children as he shut the bedroom door.

I curled up on the floor and wondered how I would get up. It wasn't about standing. It never is. It was about finding something to stand for. I didn't know, until I was knocked down, that it was me who I couldn't love. I thought I could be the nice man with the crazy family, but it turned out *I was the crazy family*. I thought the story was about loving others, and perhaps it was, but it was also how even the craziest people are worthy of love. It was about how I deserved to be loved, despite all my flaws. It was about how I did *not* deserve to be mistreated, even after all my mistakes.

When I did make it to my feet, I found I was still disoriented. I didn't like giving up on people, and I didn't like the idea of running away into the hidden world of battered women's shelters. But I didn't know if we were safe, either, and it had crossed my mind that he might one day, maybe one day soon, end up killing me, either by accident or on purpose.

I didn't know what the right decision was, so I tried not to make any decision until the last possible moment. Instead of packing up and leaving, taking my babies somewhere safe, I stayed and waited for his mania to diminish into a predictable depression, knowing that then he was more of a danger to himself than to us.

I was just out of the shower one afternoon and was examining the bruises on my face and body, thankful that the swelling on the side of my head had finally subsided. I was about to swing the mirror flat when my eyes caught something on one of the inside shelves. It was a pregnancy test.

Why not, I thought to myself as I unwrapped the white stick. Three panic-ridden minutes later, ClearBlue informed me I was going to have a baby.

I expected to feel a lot of things, but what I felt was a surprising wave of relief. Relief because I knew this meant I wouldn't be hit again. Relief because my self-worth was linked to my role as a mother and I loved my body only when there was a baby inside it. Relief and a little bit of sadness, because I knew the time for hard choices had come.

CHAPTER TWENTY

The Wall

I found the father of my soon-to-be three children in the corner of our unfinished basement, where he had been sitting for four days. I presented the positive pregnancy test like an award. He looked up with red-rimmed eyes and said "You look happy about this."

"I am happy," I told him.

So was he. He popped out of the corner and announced he was going to refinish the basement. He was also going to get a job and build a new crib from pine scraps. He was also pretty sure we needed a puppy.

It made my heart ache. There is something beautiful about this type of mania, the whirring mind of someone so happy that they must do and make and plan all things at once.

There is also something terrifying about it, the unstoppable drive to create an environment that matches the chaos within.

I didn't like the idea of medication, of the slow, sleepy brain that was well-behaved and silent. But as I watched him spin around, my own anxiety overtook me, and I knew one of us had better take some pills. I found the help I needed in my doctor. After listening to my baby's heartbeat and checking my blood pressure, she asked me what I was worried about.

"Well," I began, "I have this voice in my head that sometimes talks to me. It tells me to be calm and encourages me to love others."

"It could be worse," my doctor said. I knew she was right. For most of my life I'd had a voice in my head that told me to be afraid and to hate everyone.

"And another thing." I continued, "I'm dating someone who is bipolar and not on medication, we're both unemployed, I have two children already and I'm pretty sure I'm about to be single."

"So he's a douche," my doctor said, writing me a prescription for Zoloft.

I felt like I had found a friend.

I took a pill and waited. I took a pill every day for two weeks, and for two weeks I waited. Then one day I woke up.

It was like a ceaseless, cracking, cackling radio station in my mind had suddenly been turned off. I looked around my life, saw messes that needed to be cleaned up, and I was finally able to focus. I went from not being able to make one solitary decision to making a lot of decisions very quickly.

I tore through the house and threw away every half-finished project. I encouraged my significant other to look for work far up North as I packed his bags. When he got hired, a surprise to both of us, I waved goodbye from our front step and then went back inside and started packing my own things. I didn't know how or when, but we were leaving.

I quit smoking. I started eating. I slept through the night and started saving for a vehicle. When my rib healed, I cleared out the basement and gave all my ex's clothes to Goodwill. I was starting to feel like a boss.

Now that I could hear myself think without emotions taking over, I had some questions that needed answering. I was planning to climb out of my pit, carrying my babies on my back, but I needed to know – how did I get into this hole in the first place? What had gone wrong?

If you want to heal old wounds, sometimes you have to go back to the battlefield, God answered. *Maybe if you retrace your steps, you'll see something you missed.*

Nope. That was not what I wanted to do. Not at all. I ignored this advice as I searched online for new apartments. Except it wasn't advice. It wasn't a casual suggestion. It was a map to help me navigate the next event in my life, which started with an email.

> *Dear B,*
>
> *I just got off the phone with an old friend, someone has been trying to track you down. It seems that the foreign man you used to babysit for has harmed his daughter, and he recently confessed to his wife not just what he did to their child, but also what he did to you when you were the same age. She wanted to say she was sorry. Can I give her your number? She's moving into a women's shelter and might not be able to call for a while. Let me know.*
>
> *Love Mom*

I put my head down on the keyboard and howled. I sobbed and cried until I had no more tears left, then I laughed until I was exhausted. "I'm so glad I'm not crazy," I said to the empty room, and I really was. I never knew how much self-doubt I'd carried around until that moment. It had really happened, and he had remembered it. I wasn't alone with that memory anymore. I didn't need to wonder if I had made it up. I didn't need to question the sadness and fear that had plagued me afterwards. I had been scared *for a reason.* In fact, every crazy thing I had done back then had made *sense.*

I braced myself for a wave of emotions, for my own weakness, but it never came. I've never been more grateful for medication. Instead of the rage and anger I thought was coming, there was something new instead. It was compassion. Not for him, but for her. For his wife.

She disappeared with her daughter and I never got the chance to talk to her. I don't know what she would have said, but I imagined her saying just two words: I'm sorry. I would have told her that I knew what it felt like to be sorry, that I knew what it was like to chose a blind eye, and the terrible feeling of knowing that this misstep put my precious child in danger. I would tell her of the strength I saw in her, that in the midst of her pain and sorrow she had made it a priority to seek me out. I would tell her that hearing my truth being spoken by someone else had helped me, because I knew now that I wasn't alone, and I would tell her that she was not alone, either. I would tell her how I hoped she and her daughter got the help they needed. I would have said "I forgive you."

It was one week later that I found myself sitting in church, listening to the pastor talk about Life Groups. "Imagine doing life with other people" he said. The strange thing was, I could imagine it. I hadn't had friends in a very long time and this wasn't the first time I wondered what it might be like to have friends who would want to live my crazy life alongside of me. What would it do to my growing family if I was brave enough to have friends, friends who might hurt me, but friends who might also be a part of my story?

I signed up for a mid-week group, but then decided not to go. I wrote out a list of reasons why Bible Studies were a bad idea. I looked at that list and saw "what if this" and "maybe that" and I knew that the list was a real problem. I saw people as a collection of scary ifs and maybes. And what would they think of me if they knew me? Maybe we were all broken. Maybe we were all worth it, too.

Being brave doesn't mean you won't get hurt. It means you get out there despite the risks and you stand up despite the pain, God said. God sure did have a lot of good advice.

So I showed up. I arrived to find that the group had been incorrectly advertised as a Bible Study, when in fact it was more like an assortment of college friends and their spouses who happened to attend the same church and enjoyed meeting after work for coffee and good company. It wasn't until the food had been eaten and the kids went downstairs with the babysitter that the group moved in a more serious direction.

I entered the living room as if I was entering into a world I'd long ago walked away from, only this time I wasn't the babysitter, I was the mom upstairs.

I waited for alarm bells and red flags, but there were none. People appeared normal and level-headed. I claimed a spot on the couch and went ahead with my plan of making friends. I started awkward conversations, trying to avoid mentioning jail, drugs, crime, or unemployment.

With no current life stories I was willing to share, my conversations turned to my childhood as a missionary and my young church life.

When I said these things out loud, I recognized these stories as my own, but they were stories I didn't realize still belonged to me. I realized with a shock that I was talking about my past without feeling like I was talking about another person. It was as if my old life had suddenly merged with the present. I felt as if my story was no longer separate pieces but was slowly becoming a part of me, like I was being remade with all the broken parts of my life. And I was surprised to find that I didn't hate it, not even a little bit.

I wasn't the only one who was revisiting the past. My children's father had been coming home on weekends to spend time with the girls, and I noticed that over time he, too, was changing. He stopped showing up in work clothes. He started bringing suitcases full of toys. One weekend, he pulled up in a limo, wearing a suit and carrying a briefcase full of cell phones and vodka.

"He sure cleans up nice!" My neighbor told me as she walked by, her Chihuahua in one hand and a cigarette in the other. I couldn't agree. He may have looked nice, but I'd spent enough time as an addict to recognize a drug dealer when I saw one.

When his new girlfriend showed up, I knew for sure. I took one look at her and knew this woman hadn't eaten in a while, so I made her dinner and tried to convince her to go back home and sleep.

"I can't sleep, I'm stripping tonight," she told me between bites.

"Well you can sleep here if you promise not to have sex," I replied.

She looked at me like I knew nothing.

"I don't know how you do it," she said sadly.

"Oh honey. I take the right medication." I told her.

He went back to work at the end of that weekend, and as I watched them leave I wondered how much longer he would have a paycheck. I sighed. I'd just been added as a beneficiary to his employee healthcare, too.

When he called midweek to inform me that he thought he made more money doing crime and that the nine-to-five workday was really dragging him down, I was not surprised.

"Look on the bright side, babe." He mused. "I'll have more time to spend with you and the girls. And I'll be home for Christmas."

Click. He hung up.

Maybe now is a good time to talk about boundaries, God said. *Some type of people respect a fence, some type of people respect a wall.*

Boundaries. Of course. There are times in life when "No, thank you" or "Please, don't" are not enough, but boundaries weren't my strength. I didn't know if I'd ever had personal boundaries.

I, myself, do not like walls. I don't even like closed doors. I'd grown up in a cage and run away only to end up in a concrete cell. I knew this was not a fence-building situation, but I didn't want to put a new wall up around me and my children.

So I put up a wall around the person who needed it. It was a snowy evening in December when my children's father was arrested at the airport, with suitcases full of drugs and stolen credit cards. My own father called me from work the next morning after he had read the paper. Once again we were front page news. I'd come to hate reading about my life in the newspaper, but this time I didn't care. What appeared to be a fraying rope to onlookers, seemed to me like a bow atop the greatest Christmas present. Freedom.

The last time my children saw their father, he'd been high out of his mind and had promised them the best Christmas of their lives. I couldn't give them everything he promised, but I tried. All the money I'd saved up for a vehicle, I spent on Christmas presents and activities. I filled our holiday so full of things to do they didn't even know he wasn't there.

It was a Christmas filled with toys instead of people, bought with money I shouldn't have spent, but my relationship had swerved and skidded and grated against the pavement for years before coming to a stop at the end of a long road, and my children and I had walked away unscathed. I was a little bit panicky, a little bit anxious, but mostly grateful, and also proud.

Building walls is not for the weak. Boundaries are hard.

CHAPTER TWENTY-ONE

Team Granholm

Being a single parent is also hard. I had parented alone before, but I'd never felt single. Now I had to give up on the fantasy of a two parent family, of the life I wanted for my girls. I had to grieve the loss of my ideals, to accept the fact that things had gone the way I always knew they could but hoped they wouldn't. I had to get over it fast, too, because I was now the solitary adult in a house with two, soon to be three, children, and I was all they had. Team Granholm was solely my responsibility.

I was determined to make it. I believed that with a lot of hard work and many little steps, things were going to work out for us. I had to have hope, or else I would be crushed. I needed to believe, or else I would have given up. I needed God to remind me of who I was and all that I had overcome, to assure me that I could keep climbing.

As my due date approached, I started to sweat, and it wasn't just hormones. It was anxiety. I needed a crib and baby clothes, and I still needed a vehicle. I was back on welfare and I was really beginning to wish I hadn't spent my savings at Christmas.

When my Life Group ended a meeting by asking for prayer requests, I mentioned I was looking for a very cheap, very reliable car that could fit three child car seats. For good measure, I went home and prayed about it myself. I took all my fears and turned them into a prayer.

I needed so many things. Practical things. Basic things. Some impractical, complicated things. Mostly, I needed to know it was going to be okay.

I'm on Team Granholm, too, said God, *It's going to be okay.*

I wanted to believe this, so I kept on doing what I had been doing. Showing up. When I showed up at Life Group wearing maternity jeans from the second hand store, with the broken strap tied around my pregnant belly to keep them from falling, my dear friends asked me if there was anything I needed. Maternity clothes, maybe?

The women of my Life Group didn't tell me in loving ways that I should have made better choices. They didn't care for me by quoting scriptures or by making me feel like less because my childrens' father was in prison, which they, too, had read in the paper. They didn't do what I thought Christian women would do.

They did what sisters would do. They marched past my messy life and into my home. They brought me a whole closet full of maternity clothes, more clothes than I had ever owned. They brought a crib and baby clothes to last my baby until age four. They brought diapers and food and they brought love, the kind of love that turns over and nourishes the soil in the garden of your heart.

When my water broke, I wasn't scared. I was excited. Life for my little family had never been better. I called my mother to chat. I texted my friends. I swept the kitchen and then took a shower. I blow-dried my hair and waited for my contractions to start. I waited for an hour, but there was nothing except for an irritating backache. Finally, I called my father who dropped me off at the hospital entrance and then took my girls to his house for the night.

I sat in the waiting room of the busy maternity ward reading magazines, waiting to be admitted. I felt like this was going to be a pretty great night. The pain had escalated to a mild discomfort, which seemed like a good indication. When my number was called I bounced to the desk and informed them I was in labor.

They examined me and told me I would have to go back home and come back in the morning.

"Busses don't run this late and I'm not taking a cab across the city," I replied coolly. "I'm not leaving this hospital until I have a baby."

The nurses rolled their eyes and sent me back to the waiting room. I should have known then that we would not be friends. I found a more comfortable chair and flipped open my magazine. That is when my labor began.

It was a fire. My contractions started at three minutes apart and tore through my body. I took a breath only to scream. Blinded by the pain, I leaned against the wall and kicked and thrashed until it was over. I barely had time to complain before another wave came.

"I need an epidural! I need morphine! I need my doctor! I need PAIN MEDICATION" I screeched at all the bewildered people in the waiting room. I didn't stop there. I told the people in the hallway. I told the receptionist. I told the nurse who tried to hold me down to examine me again.

"Are you the anesthetist?" I asked the pregnant woman in the bed next to mine. When she didn't answer I continued, "Well, do you have morphine?"

When the nurse told me, in a very sad voice, that I was too dilated to get an epidural, I went into a frenzy.

"LIAR!" I yelled between contractions. "You JUST tried to send me home!"

"Get her into a room," someone behind the curtain said, and I was wheeled away into a dimly-lit room and told to relax. I kicked and screamed and tried to get off the bed. I held onto the railings as the pain ripped through my body and burned the edges of my brain.

I'd never given birth without medication before. I had never known that pain at this magnitude was a possibility. Had I known, I would never have had children. Yet there I was, in an unstoppable, all-consuming fire and my doctor was not going to make it to the hospital in time to help me. The understaffed maternity ward was not going to give me a nurse to hold my hand. I was going to be alone.

At some point, I realized this. I knew that physical relief was not coming. I knew that practical help was not coming. I knew that it was just me and this pain, and the poor nurse whom I had continually threatened, who had to remain at the end of my bed to notify the doctor when the baby's head appeared.

It's hard to think when your body is on fire and you are one contraction away from a complete breakdown, but from somewhere inside of me came a voice. It wasn't God. God knew not to try to talk to me right then.

It was a different voice. It was strong and fearless and in control. It was the voice of a warrior.

The warrior voice told me to sit still on the bed and to grip the railings. It told me to breathe and to listen to my body, because it was almost time to push. It told me to watch the clock and count. My contractions were one minute apart now, and I was going to need to focus.

When the pain changed and my body reacted, the warrior voice told me not to fight it. This was the end and I had to trust my body. The warrior voice told me when it was time to push, and when the doctor came she organized everything for my baby's arrival and commented on my control. I didn't respond because I was busy listening for the voice inside myself.

Nobody had to tell me the moment my son was born. I was paying attention this time. I said the only words I ever said to the doctor who delivered my last baby: "Hand him to me."

I took his naked, sticky body, the umbilical cord still attached to me, and put him on top of my own naked, sticky body. He smelled my sweat and my tears, he felt my heartbeat, he felt my strength and my joy, and he knew that he was home. I held my baby, whose heart was beating with my blood, and I knew that I could do anything.

I wish I'd known that with my girls. I wish I'd been awake and paying attention. I wish I had taken them right away and held them against my skin, instead of watching from a bed, watching another adult give my new baby a bath, measuring and changing her before handing my daughter to me. I wish I hadn't been afraid of pain, I wish I'd known that I could ignore everyone and everything and just focus on myself.

But I didn't know until I was forced to be a mother without medication and without help. I didn't know until I had my son. Then I knew. The warrior was me.

Out of the deep well of my being the warrior had risen. It was the warrior that had prompted me to move across the country with my children. It was the warrior who had chosen to stay instead of run away. It was the warrior that could take on ugly beasts, even the beasts inside of me, and tear them down. It was the warrior that could build walls and it was the warrior who was stronger than the pain of childbirth.

I left the hospital the next day, on a Thursday afternoon. The upcoming weekend was Easter Weekend, so I had a dinner to plan and I wanted to leave the hospital in time to grocery shop. On Sunday I dressed my girls and my new baby, and took them to church, showing off my little man to my Life Group friends.

"Can we bring you dinner tomorrow?" two of my friends asked. As a rule, I never turn down free food or guests who plan ahead, so I happily agreed.

They brought dinner, delicious turkey chili, enough to feed twenty people. Which turned out to be a good thing, because twenty people showed up. My entire Life Group showed up. Everybody loves a new baby.

My Life Group friends also loved surprises. I was called to my front door and when I swung it open, there in front of my house was a minivan with a big red bow.

Do you know how God answers prayers? With people. Do you know how God shows you you're loved? With people. Do you know how to feel safe and valued and worthy? Find your people.

My people answered my prayers. They loved me. They valued me. They believed I was worthy of great things. They heard me when I said I needed a vehicle, and they hunted high and low for the perfect one. And they thought I might worry about expenses, so they paid for a year of insurance and gave me an envelope full of cash for vehicle maintenance.

I was overwhelmed with gratitude and happiness, and my friends, the ones who had taken from their savings and their own grocery money to put towards this amazing gift, were also happy. They poured out their love and I took it with both hands, and we were all filled.

My life has been full of things I never thought would happen, and I had learned to fear the unpredictable. But the truth is, not all surprises are bad. Not all people will hurt you. Sometimes great, amazing things happen, and learning how to accept good things is just as important as learning how to accept bad things.

Loving other people changed me, but learning to let others love me changed me, too. The van became more than vehicle, it became a sacrament. It became love that I could touch with my hands. It became grace, a grace that saw that the best I could do was show up to a Bible Study week after week, and rewarded me for being brave enough. It became a joy, a joy which taught me that under angry tears and sad tears there was another well spring, a waterfall of happiness.

I cried happy tears when I buckled my children in their car seats. I cried happy tears at stop signs and red lights. I cried happy tears when I saw my car keys sitting on the kitchen counter. I cried, and it was not a weakness. It was strength.

It had been a long time since I'd had my own vehicle. When you're sixteen and you get your first car, it means freedom. When you're twenty-nine and you get your first van, it can mean freedom, too, especially if you were on house arrest.

Once I'd been to all the places I could drive to in one day, I started thinking about driving to the coast. My children had never been on vacation, and I wanted to take them to the ocean. I wanted to head west until I could see nothing but blue stretch before me. I wanted to feel sand and breathe the salty air. I lived on the west side of the city and I knew that one road and a thousand miles was all that stood between my house and the ocean.

Some people plan for a vacation, they save and prepare. I am not one of those people. I could have saved for years and still not have had enough money to pay bills and take a trip. Travelling with three kids and no money seemed like an adventure. My parents never regretted travelling with an infant, and the idea didn't scare me, either. I'd lived out of a suitcase more than once in my life. I'd heard someone say once that you have to know where you come from to know where you're going, and I thought about this a lot. Maybe I could go back and figure out where I had come from, who I had been, and who I might be if I discovered my strengths. The idea grew on me.

It grew until it wasn't just an idea anymore, it was an obsession. My home held just as many bad memoires as good ones, and I liked the idea of leaving it behind. It was an idea I was afraid to tell anyone, because I suspected that I might have to return the van if my church friends found out I wanted to use their gift to leave. In the end, I figured if they really wanted it back they could have it. I would find another way to go.

When I told my Life Group friends that I was moving back to Vancouver, they did not ask for the van back. They threw me a going away party and gave me money for gas. They loved and supported me so unconditionally that they wanted the best for me, even if that meant saying goodbye. They even helped me pack.

I headed out onto the highway on a hot summer evening with three kids, a goldfish, and the red sunset lighting up the road ahead. We were going on a very long vacation.

The Van, 2012

CHAPTER TWENTY-TWO

The End

I drove until I reached the shores of the Pacific Ocean. Then I drove onto a ferry, arrived on Vancouver Island, and drove some more. I didn't stop until I could stand in one spot and see all the places I had called home – the United States, Canada, and the wide open sea.

I walked my life backwards, bringing my children with me, giving them my favorite memories to keep for themselves and stopping every once in a while to pick up a part of me that I had left behind. To move forward, to move towards wholeness, I first had to go back and collect myself, the bits and pieces of me that I had abandoned because I was too ashamed to call them my own. It was a broken path, but I had my two best friends, God and Zoloft, to help me find my way, and I had my three babies to remind me why I needed to take this journey.

I started with the broken pieces of me I'd left at church. I'd been raised to see the church as a place of authority, the final word on morality and sin and judgment. I'd grown up and realized that was backwards, that the church was just a beautiful building with a bunch of broken people inside. I saw Christians trying to hide their scars by pointing out the scars on others, and I saw

Christians hurting their communities and then showing up on Sunday believing they'd been forgiven. I saw that if you were the right kind of Christian, you were above suspicion or reproach, and I hated it. I hated it a lot.

I had also seen God show up in a school gymnasium. I had seen God in Christians. I had found God in my own dark places. I wondered if I might find God in a church, too. So I looked.

I went to a Pentecostal church. I went to a Baptist church. I went to an Anglican church and a United church and I even went to a Mennonite church. I went into these places looking for God, and in each church I found people I could love. None of these churches were perfect, but when I showed up looking for God, I found love, not in the church, but in myself. I thought about the day I told my parents I was no longer a Christian. I had been right to walk away – religion wasn't for me, and it might never be. But God isn't a religion. God is love, and love is everywhere. Even in a church.

I was in a Southern Baptist church, the same type of church where I first went to Sunday school in Georgia, when the pastor announced upcoming baptisms. There was no baptismal tank, no pomp or ostentatious ceremony. He was going to baptize whoever wanted to be baptized in the Pacific Ocean and live stream the event on the church's website.

I had decided against religious rituals, but something about getting baptized in the Pacific Ocean appealed to me.

The part of me that had been broken in the church was full of hate, but the hate hadn't protected me. It had just made me more broken. I couldn't keep the broken piece the way it was. Hate doesn't heal. I tried to dust it off with new experiences but sometimes old emotions are stubborn.

I stood waist-deep in water as old as time and I said goodbye to my hate. I stopped running from the Church and instead, saw it as my own. The Church had been a part of my life since the day I was born. It was my family. I couldn't leave just because I didn't like a few things. I had to stay; I had to find ways to love the people there.

I was hoping that baptism would be a spiritual experience, but instead it was a physical one. Despite the sunny day, despite the wetsuit I was wearing, I came up out of the water with a chill that turned into a three-day flu. I swallowed handfuls of Tylenol and spent fevered days and nights wishing I'd been baptized in the Anglican church the way my daughters had been, where they just sprinkle holy water on your head. But sometimes when you're dirty, you have to take a bath.

I had been back on the coast for a year when I developed what I thought was an ingenious plan to make extra money. I was still on social assistance, and finances were still tight, and the cheapest way to decorate was still painting. I walked into Benjamin Moore one day to find that half the stock was on sale. All the old oil-based paints were being cleared to make room for a new line of non-toxic paints.

I bought the old stock for one dollar a gallon. I had discovered Pinterest, so I knew just what to do with fifty-five cans of designer paint. I was going to collect free furniture from the side of the road, bring it home in my van, repair it, repaint it, and sell it.

It started off great. I sold refurbished dining room sets and desks, hutches and bookshelves. I painted when my children napped and when they went to bed at night, and during the day I would pack my children and my wares into the van and deliver it to customers.

We were on our way back from delivering a nice Santorini-blue bedside table when I saw a sign for a free couch.

I got it into my head that I was going to reupholster the couch and sell it. I had recently found giant swaths of fabric at the thrift store and sewn myself curtains, and I had a lot of extra fabric and no more windows to cover. I called the number on the sign and arranged to pick it up.

The couch may have fit into the van lengthwise if I didn't have my children with me, but I did. I was also running low on patience and common sense. The guy selling me the couch offered to strap it to the roof, but I told him not to.

"I'm too short to get it down once I get back home and I don't have anyone to help me," I reasoned.

"How are you going to get it in your house by yourself?" he asked.

"I'm stronger than I look," I told him, and I shoved the couch in across the sliding door of the van so that it balanced widthwise.

I stuffed the couch pillows around the car seats for safety, and once we were all buckled in, I headed down the highway towards our home, going five miles an hour with the hazard lights blinking, half the couch sticking out the open side door.

I was pulled over in less than ten minutes.

The officers weren't sure what to do. One of them took down my license and vehicle information while the other hummed and hawed about the couch.

"As if you've never seen someone moving furniture before!" I said, irritated.

"Well, Ma'am, the couch is un-tethered, the vehicle door is wide open, the kids are in the backseat with the wind in their faces, and you're driving down a highway slower than a turtle."

I didn't see the problem, but they told me I would have to leave the couch on the side of the road and come back to pick it up when I had a proper vehicle. I drove home fuming about lost time and lost sales.

The next morning, I got a knock on the door. I'd never transferred my license over when I came back to the coast because I had unpaid fines and parking tickets, which I didn't want to pay. The past is the past unless it's the DMV. Then it's the past, the present, and the future.

The officers had gone over their notes and had apparently gotten over the couch long enough to do some sleuthing. I'd been on the coast too long – I should have changed my license over within ninety days.

"Technically, Ma'am, your license is invalid. We're going to need to take it." I was informed. I put down my coffee and got my purse.

That license was the only piece of Canadian identification I had. The next day, I brought my American birth certificate and my Social Security Number to the Canadian DMV and tried to transfer my license, but they turned me away. I applied for a Canadian passport, but I was turned away there, too. It's hard to get new ID when you have none to start with, and I had none because I'd thrown it away after my failed suicide attempt.

I applied for a new Citizenship paper, but I was given a six-to-eight month wait time. I wouldn't be able to drive until that piece of paper came.

I had no license and I was left with a vehicle I couldn't drive. The van sat in the parking lot for a month while I took my time wondering what to do. Eventually my father pointed out that I couldn't afford to insure a vehicle I couldn't drive.

"I think you should sell it," my father advised.

"I'll never sell it. I'm going to be buried with the keys in my cold, clenched fist," I told him.

By the end of the week, it had been sold.

I am not the kind of person who values money. I like money, I need money, but I believe that money is only worth what you can buy with it, and the value of a gift is priceless. I couldn't believe that just over a year after getting the van, a day which was such a profound experience for me, one that represented love and friendship and grace, I had nothing from it but a small pile of cash.

"I'm so embarrassed," I told God. "I should never have come back here."

It's tough wanting everything to be perfect. God said.

"I should have known that my past was going to ruin everything. I can't believe I was stupid enough to throw my wallet away that day." I mumbled.

I don't remember you being stupid, God mused.

"Look, I think we can both agree that everything I did was wrong, and now I'm paying for it. This isn't just about the van. It's about the loss of something that was more. Something I won't get back. The van was part of me...it was part of my story." I felt like I shouldn't have to explain the obvious to God, of all people.

Story is an interesting word, God said.

"Well, not an actual story." I clarified. God knew that I hadn't written anything but jail mail and Facebook posts since my journal had been used in court. God knew I hated writing. Once your thoughts were on paper, people tended to get judgmental.

I wonder what you would see if you could read your own life, God said.

I do well in one-sided conversations. They seem to work out for me more often than not.

"Alright," I said to God. "Let's say I *was* going to write a story about my life, where would I start?"

Why not start at the beginning? God said, wishing that the obvious didn't have to be explained to me, after all this time.

Two things happened that day. I bought my first-ever non-stolen laptop, and I started writing this story.

The first chapter I wrote was terrible. It was awful. I wrote in third person and tried to be as detached as possible. I started by explaining events like they'd happened to someone else.

I showed my sister-friend, who read it and said "keep writing."

I wrote this book one chapter at a time, and after each chapter she said, "keep writing."

I wrote every day for three months, and slowly my writing changed. I started writing about myself. I travelled in my mind, going back into each memory and sitting there for a bit, absorbing my emotions. I felt my own pain and put words to it, sometimes for the first time. I took each heavy piece of my heart and threw it into this book, and one day I realized that I was building something. I was building my life.

I read my own story and I could see that I wasn't a collection of separate pieces. I was all the pieces of myself at once. I was *un*broken. What I had previously thought of as individual occurrences - as a misunderstood friendship, a Bible Study gone bad, a bully for a mentor, a white line, handcuffs, rogue boyfriends, and babies, they were all part of the life that had made me who I was. And I was not a sad, broken girl, as I had always thought. I was a human being.

I saw myself and I wanted to scoop up the little girl I had been and tell her how amazing she was, that it was okay to make friends and that it was okay to be cautious, too. I wanted to talk to my teenage self and let her know it was okay to be calm, that anxiety was not a friend, and that help was out there if she knew where to look. I wanted to talk to the young mother who loved her babies but couldn't look at herself in the mirror, and tell her it was okay to just be, that who she was, was enough.

When you are thinking about your own life, context is important. Knowing where you come from matters.

I lived and I got hurt. I got angry and I hurt myself, and then I hurt others. I lived a broken life because I thought that was who I was and what I deserved. But I also had strengths. I had dreams. I had hopes. When I saw only my weaknesses, I sold myself short.

When I started writing the chapter about high school, a memory hit me like a brick on the head. One of my old teachers, seeing my enthusiasm for college, said to me, "Bethany, I think you'd really enjoy university. I think you'd like the challenge."

Once I remembered it, I heard her voice over and over in my head. I couldn't let it go.

I loved being a mother, and I still do, but I had no identity outside of motherhood. I'd rebuilt my almost non-existent self-worth and my identity around having children.

Since the day I first found out I was pregnant, I thought that being a mother was my purpose, that I'd been given a second chance for this sole reason.

But what if I could do something else? What if I could finally have a resume that wasn't a lie? What if I could be good at something and make life better for my little family? What if I still belonged in society? What if I could give the world something more than a baby?

I started looking at post-secondary schools like they were somewhere I might belong.

I was researching local universities when I realized I didn't have enough identification to apply for school or to cash a student loan. I was still waiting on my Canadian citizenship. *I'll just focus on writing*, I told myself, *and everything will work out when it's supposed to work out*. No grand plan, that was the new plan.

But there was a plan. At the end of that week, I got a message from a stranger. This woman had just taken over an old optometry clinic and had found, tucked away in the back, a wallet. It was my wallet, the one I'd thrown away. The optometry clinic was just down the street from the house where I had lived when I started doing drugs. She wasn't sure why the previous owner had kept the wallet all these years, but she thought the right thing to do was return it.

I love it when people do the right thing. I gave her my address, and when my old wallet came, I took the rest of the money from the sale of the van and went, not to pay fines and get my license, but to the community college down the street. I was worried that not graduating high school would disqualify me from enrollment, but I went anyway and found that mature students don't need high school diplomas to get into college. I just took a few tests. A few weeks later, I got an acceptance letter

I thought the births of my children were amazing. I thought getting a van wrapped in a red bow was amazing. But neither of these compared to the day I found out I was going to college. I didn't know how much I wanted a future until I had one. The college acceptance letter was an invitation for me to join the world.

I didn't know until I got to school how much I would love Psychology. When I found the Social Sciences department, I found my place in the world. I found a place where an interesting past made for an interesting client. I found a place where brokenness was studied and not feared. I found that I could put my own mind together with magic of science and that I could nourish myself with a positive self-image, and I found that not only did I have the tools to help myself, but that I had the tools to help others.

School drew out my strengths, and these strengths were the glue that held my newly-mended life together. I declared Psychology as my major, English as my minor, and threw myself into my studies.

I applied for transfers to better schools in farther places. I got accepted, and like the many times before, I started packing. I explained this move to my children.

I told them that we were leaving, not to pick up the pieces of the past, but to pave the way for a future. We were leaving to follow a dream.

"Pack light," I cheerfully instructed. "We're heading out and starting over."

I made a Dream Jar and started selling all the things that couldn't fit into a suitcase. I held a week-long garage sale and at the end of it, we had just enough money for our train tickets. All we had left were clothes, toys, and textbooks, and if you knew my family, you'd know that was enough, too.

Three years after leaving the Midwest to head to the coast, I left the coast to head to the Midwest. My soul vacation was over.

Fourteen suitcases and two bikes later, we were on board the train, settling into our east-bound journey. The wheels turned and we were off into the glorious, unknown tomorrow. I watched the country roll by the window, and I said softly to myself, "I'm alive," over and over again until it became a song; the song of the unbroken. It isn't a song of perfection. It is a song of resilience. It is a song of second chances. It is a song of fear and pain and hope and love, all twisted together in beautiful ways, and held together by our beating hearts.

It's a song that is not easily unsung.

"You can lose it all

– all the things you thought

mattered most–

and rise up to tell a better story yet.

Turn it loose."

Jen Hatmaker, *Interrupted: When Jesus Wrecks Your Comfortable Christianity*

Epilogue

How could there be an end to a story like this? Life will sway and turn and follow its unknown path until the day I take my last breath. I've had a second chance for almost everything, and second chances mean each day is an unplanned blessing.

When I introduced my children into this story, it occurred to me that they might want to read this book one day. I wondered if I should I go back and change the story to make it more palatable. After some thought, I decided I would not. I wrote about events in my life as accurately as I could remember them, and although this memoir remains the perspective of one person only, there is truth here that I hope my children will recognize. I also hope that my children will be brave enough to want to know the truth, even if that truth is hard.

If my children learn anything from me, I would want it to be that there is strength in hope, there is magic in grace, and there is a transformative power in love. Yet all these things are diluted when we don't know how dead we were before we came alive. If my babies one day find themselves far from where they should be, through no fault of their own or because of all their own faults, I want them to know that they can make it back. And I don't want them to be afraid to tell their own stories. *The end is never the end.*

Photo © Bethany Granholm 2016

Bethany Granholm has an educational background in Psychology and English, and studies at the University of Manitoba. She lives in the Midwest with her three children and is addicted to Starbucks coffee and Instagram.

More at bethanygranholm.com

Facebook: bethany.granholm

Twitter and Instagram: @teamgranholm

...

Made in the USA
Charleston, SC
21 July 2016